composition STUDIES

Volume 38, Number 2

Fall 2010

Editor
Jennifer Clary-Lemon

Book Review Editor
Asao B. Inoue

Production Editor
David Elder

Editorial Assistants
Christopher Campbell
Katy Dycus
Scot Hanson
Joel Overall
Kristi Schwertfeger Serrano

Former Editors
Gary Tate
Robert Mayberry
Christina Murphy
Peter Vandenberg
Ann George
Carrie Leverenz
Brad E. Lucas

Advisory Board

Linda Adler-Kassner
Eastern Michigan University

Tom Amorose
Seattle Pacific University

Chris Anson
North Carolina State University

Valerie Balester
Texas A&M University

Robert Brooke
University of Nebraska, Lincoln

Sidney Dobrin
University of Florida

Lisa Ede
Oregon State University

Paul Heilker
*Virginia Polytechnic Institute
and State University*

James Inman
*University of Maryland
University College*

Laura Micciche
University of Cincinnati

Peggy O'Neill
Loyola College

Victor Villanueva
Washington State University

I0027754

THE UNIVERSITY OF WINNIPEG

SUBSCRIPTIONS

Composition Studies is published twice each year (May and November). Subscription rates: Individuals $25 (Domestic) and $30 (International); Institutions $75 (Domestic) and $75 (International); Students $15.

BACK ISSUES

Some back issues are available at $8 per issue. Photocopies of earlier issues are available for $3.

BOOK REVIEWS

Assignments are made from a file of potential book reviewers. To have your name added to the file, send a current vita to the Book Review Editor at asao@inoueweb.com.

SUBMISSIONS

All appropriate essay submissions will be blind reviewed by two external readers. Manuscripts should be 3,500-7,500 words and conform to current MLA guidelines for format and documentation; they should be free of author's names and other identifying references. *Electronic submissions are preferred*: consult our Web site for details. (For print submissions, submit three titled, letter-quality copies with a cover letter including the title and author contact information, loose postage sufficient to mail manuscripts to two reviewers, and a #10 SASE for the return of reviewer comments.) *Composition Studies* will not consider previously published manuscripts. We discourage the submission of conference papers that have not been revised or extended for a critical reading audience. Those wishing to submit Course Designs should first consult our Web site for specific instructions. Letters to the editor and responses to articles are strongly encouraged.

Direct all correspondence to:

Jennifer Clary-Lemon, Editor
Department of Rhetoric, Writing, and Communications
University of Winnipeg
515 Portage Avenue Winnipeg, MB R3B 2E9
Canada

Composition Studies is grateful for the generous support of the Dean of Arts and the Department of Rhetoric, Writing, and Communications at the University of Winnipeg.

ISSN 1534-9322

www.compositionstudies.uwinnipeg.ca

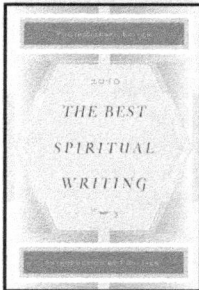

Reviewers

All essay submissions are reviewed blind by two external readers; those listed below are members of the active reader pool. We thank them for their critical contributions to scholarship in the field.

Linda Adler-Kassner
Tom Amorose
Valerie Balester
Cheryl Ball
Nicholas Behm
Patricia Belanoff
Patricia Bizzell
Bill Bolin
Darsie Bowden
Colin Brooke
Robert Brooke
Nancy Buffington
Beth Burmester
Paul Butler
Mary Ann Cain
Carol Lea Clark
Kirsti Cole
Lisa Coleman
James Comas
Juanita Rodgers Comfort
Thomas Deans
Jane Detweiler
Ronda Leathers Dively
Sidney Dobrin
Whitney Douglas
Donna Dunbar-Odom
Lynell Edwards
David Elder
Janet Carey Eldred
Michelle Eodice
Heidi Estrem
Sheryl Fontaine
Helen Fox
Tom Fox
Christy Friend
Richard Fulkerson
Catherine Gabor

Lynée Lewis Gaillet
Alice Gilliam
Maureen Daly Goggin
Angela González
Lorie Goodman
Heather Brodie Graves
Roger Graves
Paul Hanstedt
Dana Harrington
Jeanette Harris
Cynthia Haynes
Paul Heilker
Carl Herndl
Anne Herrington
Brooke Hessler
Charlotte Hogg
Bruce Horner
Rebecca Moore Howard
Sue Hum
Brian Huot
James Inman
Asao Inoue
Rebecca Jackson
T. R. Johnson
Judith Kearns
Martha Kruse
bonnie kyburz
Mary Lamb
Joe Law
Donna LeCourt
Neal Lerner
Carrie Leverenz
Min-Zhan Lu
Brad Lucas
William Macauley
Tim Mayers

Lisa McClure
Dan Meltzer
Laura Rose Micciche
Susan Miller
Ruth Mirtz
Clyde Moneyhun
Roxanne Mountford
Gerald P. Mulderig
Joan A. Mullin
Joddy Murray
Marshall Myers
Gerald Nelms
Jon Olson
Peggy O'Neill
Derek Owens
Irv Peckham
Donna Qualley
Ellen Quandahl
Kelly Ritter
Randall Roorda
Blake Scott
Ellen Schendel
Carol Severino
Wendy Sharer
Steve Sherwood
Donna Strickland
Peter Vandenberg
Deirdre Vinyard
Zachary Waggoner
Kathleen Welch
Nancy Welch
Thomas West
Katherine Wills
Rosemary Winslow
Vershawn Ashanti Young
Janet Zepernick

(CELJ)

Member of the Council of Editors of Learned Journals

composition STUDIES

Volume 38, Number 2

Fall 2010

articles

course design

book reviews

Teaching the Analytical Life

Brian Jackson

Using a survey of 138 writing programs, I argue that we must be more explicit about what we think students should get out of analysis to make it more likely that students will transfer their analytical skills to different settings. To ensure our students take analytical skills with them at the end of the semester, we must simplify the task we assign and teach deliberately for transfer. If we can teach students to evaluate rather than just interpret an argument, we will teach them to be citizen-critics engaging in public debate over the merits of arguments about issues that influence us all.

"I wonder if you people aren't a bit too—well, strong, on the virtues of analysis. I mean, once you've taken it all apart, fine, I'll be first to applaud your industry. But other than a lot of bits and pieces lying about, what have you said?"
—Roger Mexico, in Thomas Pynchon's *Gravity's Rainbow* (88)

I. The Analytical Life

It is very likely that at some point this semester, most of us who teach writing will tell our students to go find something to analyze. We might give them books filled with speeches, essays, articles, and images—anthologized, commercially-packaged, and waiting to be vivisected. Or we may send students into the world of commercial messages, political speeches, poems, artwork, Web sites, and films and tell them to choose, from that cacophony, a single artifact upon which to inflict a new and often Greek-sounding taxonomy of interpretation. Sometimes we mandate a single text. ("This semester we will analyze the film *Crash*.") Sometimes we tell students to analyze their own souls.

Like the research paper, the analysis is one of the most popular school genres for the first-year writing course, and, like the research paper, it flourishes by the weight of its own tacit tradition. As an evolutionary product of literary and rhetorical criticism, analysis has become so much a part of the curriculum that we hardly know it's there. Its purpose goes without saying; we all know why we assign analysis, so why talk about it? The tacit-ness of the genre is evident in the professional literature where the only reliable place in the last fifty years we find helpful specifics about *teaching* analysis is the textbooks and handbooks. It seems as a discipline that we have moved on to other concerns. However, since most of us teach analysis in some form or another, we might want to deliberate more about why we teach our most popular genre.

Arguing for analysis is picking the low fruit; its importance, it seems, is self-evident. The power to analyze is one of those "trained capacities" John Dewey speaks of that helps students understand, evaluate, or resist the never-ending stream of commercial, political, institutional, and social messages that pummel them twenty-four hours a day (Dewey, *The Early Works* 5: 76). We analyze texts to understand, appreciate, or defend ourselves. In a metacognitive sense, our analytical skills (or lack thereof) often determine our quality of life in concrete ways. Analysis comes into play in both the prosaic and the profound: when we consumers get a bill we don't understand or a contract with small print; when campaign committees and comedians look over speech transcripts of political adversaries; when lawyers pore over Supreme Court decisions and tax accountants study the tax code; when old widows and widowers receive mail from faux charities and scams; when voters read propositions and referenda; when college students get scolding e-mails from parents and ambiguous text messages from romantic interests; when we want to understand or appreciate a text or artifact or event more deeply than we already do. Sometimes we perform analysis when it seems our love lives, careers, finances, or way of life is at stake in the interpretation and/or evaluation of a document. As Gerald Graff has argued, the intellectual life is the analytical life (*Clueless* 96-7).

At least this is the sales pitch our students get when it comes time to analyze "Once More to the Lake" once more. It is a good pitch, all things considered. In essence we promise students that what they learn from us will go with them to other contexts and give them power in their personal, professional, and public lives—power, more specifically, to analyze texts (e.g., newspaper articles, presidential speeches, advertisements, popular films) to determine their merits and demerits. Are we delivering on this promise? Are we teaching the analytical life? Or is the analytical essay a "school genre," as David Smit argues, that often does not "really convey any information to anyone who needs the information, nor really try to persuade anyone of any particular viewpoint" (165)? Since provisional survey data suggest that analysis is the central component of first-year writing, we should, as Elizabeth Wardle recommends, engage the transfer issue and come to terms with this pervasive genre (66). If we want analysis to be more than "just practice" (Smit 165), we must be more explicit about what we think students should get out of it. We should also simplify the task of analysis to make it more likely that students will transfer their analytical skills to different settings.

II. Analysis in the Undergraduate Curriculum

Dictionary definitions of *analysis* invoke an act of dissection—pulling something apart to see what it's made of, to see how it is composed. To analyze is to determine how the parts make the whole or how the whole fits into a bigger whole. In the writing program where I work, graduate students teach the general concept of analysis to FYC students by dumping out the contents of a backpack, supposedly left in the room by a student from a previous class, and asking students to infer from the contents what the owner is like. Analysis is a standard skill for any discipline, any profession, any intelligent way of life, and since it is such a broad, generalizable skill we find different interpretations of what it is, what it's worth, and how to teach it.

In English Studies, analysis is a reading skill. Adler and van Doren call analysis a third-level reading skill, after elementary (essential literacy) and inspectional (prereading, skimming, etc.) reading. Analysis involves—or at least *can* involve—classifying a text, situating it in a context, discovering its structure, decoding its terms, laying bare its strategies, revealing its argument, and (in some instances) evaluating its worth (Adler and van Doren 59). To complicate matters, advances in New Media Studies and visual rhetoric make analysis less an act of *literacy* than of *semiotics* (Kress and van Leeuwen 19-20). At any rate, the only way to find out whether students know how to do this is to get them to write their reading, which makes analysis a composing skill as well. English students in the 1880s wrote analyses in the very first freshman composition courses taught by Adams Sherman Hill, who hoped, together with his boss, Francis James Child, Professor of Rhetoric at Harvard, that students "would acquire a taste for good reading" by doing so (Brereton 48). Harvard's entering freshmen took written examinations that required them to "discuss the rhetorical qualities" or "give [their] opinion of the literary worth" of passages from writers like Milton, Defoe, Pope, Hawthorne, and Longfellow (Brereton 441). Mimesis was a secondary goal: by analyzing great writing, Hill's students would adopt "better forms of expression" (Brereton 48). Likewise, in his *Handbook of Rhetorical Analysis*, published in 1891, John Genung introduced students to the "science" of analysis as the only true way "to make, or to discover, [their] own rhetoric" by studying good models (Genung vii). In fact, for most of the history of teaching rhetoric *analysis* was not necessarily an act of interpretation but a process students went through to learn to appreciate and imitate exemplary texts (see Clark; Fahnestock and Secor 178; Gross and Keith).

It is likely, and unsurprising, that compositionists teach interpretive analysis so pervasively in first-year writing because of our professional interests in literary and rhetorical criticism. We teach analysis often because we "do" analysis, in some way or another, for a living. More accurately, we do history, theory, and criticism; freshmen do analysis. (If they go on to study in English or Communication, they have a 6% or 13% chance, respectively, of taking upper-division courses in rhetorical theory or criticism. If they major in English, they'll have at least a 70% chance to take a course in literary theory or criticism; around 40% are required to take such a course. See Jackson 193; Huber.) It is just as likely that analysis plays such a leading role in the curriculum out of pedagogical necessity, or inertia. Close reading practices evolved at the turn of the twentieth century in the newly-minted English departments where students came "face to face with the work itself," in the words of Indiana's chair of English in 1895 (Graff, *Professing* 123). Criticism—close reading—was meant to be liberating for students. No longer did they have to muddle through histories or biographies or etymologies; neither did the teachers. "Given the vast unknowns on both sides of the lectern," writes Gerald Graff, reflecting on his experience as an amateur teacher, "'the work itself' was indeed our salvation" (Graff, *Professing* 179). In reality, the "work itself" has never been fully sufficient for student writers. Instructors teach vocabularies fixed by research interests in poetics, linguistics, rhetoric, argumentation, philosophy, semiotics, and cultural studies to load the toolbox that students are asked to lug with them to the text. A mixture of professional interests, curricular history, and program necessity has kept analysis in composition whether it continues to be useful or not.

In spite of the critique that analysis is a school practice, it is clear that we value it as a cognitive skill that potentially transfers to new situations, even if the analysis paper, like Spam, does not exist in the natural world. In 1981, analysis was "the most frequent kind of school writing" in grade school, according to Applebee's influential study (qtd. in Hillocks 58). Tracking university-level writing, the National Survey of Student Engagement (NSSE), in cooperation with The Council of Writing Program Administrators, discovered in their 2008 survey of 23,000 students that "the most common writing tasks were to analyze something or argue a position" ("Promoting Engagement" 21). NSSE categorized analysis as a "higher-order writing" activity, along with summarization and argument, and reported that both first-year students and seniors analyzed or evaluated something in 91% of the papers they wrote (22). This evidence suggests that in spite of Smit's argument that analysis is a school (i.e. artificial) genre written in isolation of real needs and situations, most first-year and university writing programs value and teach it anyway. The reason for this is not hard to puzzle out. As my survey discussion that follows suggests, writing teachers and administrators seem to believe that we can acclimate students to the cognitive process of analysis in all its intricacy by assigning students to do it as calisthenics for future analytical acts. Amy Devitt has argued convincingly that we salvage first-year writing from obsolescence in part by seeing the analytical essay as an "antecedent" genre that students can draw from when they need to analyze artifacts in their own fields as majors, which again, according to the NSSE, they do in 91% of their writing as seniors (202).

III. Our Favorite Assignment: A Survey

To get a better sense of how analysis pervades the curriculum, in Winter 2009 my research assistants, Ty Campbell and Jalena Reschke, and I administered an online survey to which 138 writing program administrators and first-year writing instructors responded. We targeted a sample of colleges and universities from the Carnegie Foundation's nine categories of bachelor-granting institutions, from baccalaureate colleges to research-intensive institutions. Since we could not always find writing program administrators, particularly in the baccalaureate and liberal arts colleges, we asked first-year writing instructors from these institutions to respond. Of the 138 responses we received, 105 identified their institutional affiliation: roughly 36% (38 schools) identified as baccalaureate colleges, 36% as masters colleges and universities (38), and 27% as research universities (29), according to the Carnegie Foundation classifications. Though I cannot argue that our sample is technically representative of national practice, I believe the responses we received suggest trends across the board in first-year writing programs. In the survey, 92% of respondents said they assign students to perform analysis in FYC (see Table 1); 78% assign it more than once, and of that group we found dozens who assign three or more analyses to first-year students. These numbers seem to reinforce the NSSE findings that analysis is trendy in the university curriculum. Even the research paper is not as popular in first-year writing. According to our survey, 80% of programs and instructors assign research writing in the first year.

Analysis	92%
Research paper	80%
Opinion paper (e.g., editorial or other argumentative essay)	75%
Personal writing (e.g., narrative or personal essay)	55%
Blog, wiki, Web page, or other online writing	17%
Creative writing (e.g., fiction, drama, or poetry)	8%
Other*	26%

Table 1 : *What major writing assignments are your first-year students required to complete? Mark all that apply.*
   * A few answers: visual analysis, ad analysis, critical inquiry, article analysis, evaluative paper, contextual analysis, "we don't

necessarily call it anything particular," "no program—we all do our own thing."

Names for analysis assignments vary, and each name suggests a possibly unique theoretical approach to the proto-genre. Table 2 indicates that the most popular title is "rhetorical analysis," with "analysis" and "critical analysis" coming in second and third. We did not refine our research tool enough to reveal whether respondents would have considered other terms as synonymous. For example, it would be interesting to know if someone who assigns a "textual analysis" would consider a rhetorical, critical, or discourse analysis the same thing. Would analysis by any other name smell as sweet? I assume that in spite of whatever similarities they might have, rhetorical analysis is not the same as literary analysis which is not the same as textual analysis, though they might share similar cognitive processes.

Rhetorical Analysis	51%
Analysis	46%
Critical Analysis	44%
Textual Analysis	34%
Literary Analysis	28%
Close Reading	28%
Cultural Analysis	17%
Discourse Analysis	8%

Table 2: *What does your program call the analysis assignment(s)? Mark all that apply.*

If our respondents represent the rest of us, then we teach analysis for a variety of purposes, with a few trends worth noting. We found that 84% of our respondents said that it was "very important" to teach students how to evaluate an argument in terms of its strengths and weaknesses (see Table 3). The second most popular purpose for analysis was to teach students how to evaluate the effectiveness of an argument in terms of its context, audience, and original purpose. These two data suggest the endurance of rhetoric as theoretical grounds for teaching composition, in spite of those who continue to argue that they have nothing in common, or at least shouldn't. Table 3 also reveals that at least 32% of respondents consider it "not important" to teach students to appreciate the aesthetic value of a text. Apparently writing teachers and program administrators favor the pragmatic value of teaching students how to evaluate the strength of an argument in its rhetorical situation over teaching them how to read like liberal humanists appraising artistic merit, which is, we suggest, another sign that rhetoric reigns in first-year comp (and probably nowhere else in most English departments).

Purpose	Not Important	Somewhat Important	Very Important
To teach students how to interpret texts correctly through close reading	10 (8%)	32 (26%)	**82 (66%)**
To teach students how to appreciate a text's aesthetic value	40 (32%)	**63 (50%)**	22 (18%)
To teach students how to evaluate an argument in terms of its strengths and weaknesses	4 (3%)	17 (14%)	**103 (83%)**
To teach students how to evaluate the effectiveness of an argument in terms of its context, audience, and original purpose	4 (3%)	21 (17%)	**100 (80%)**
To prepare students for critical civic engagement	17 (14%)	**58 (46%)**	50 (40%)
To help students develop their own rhetorical skill through imitation	16 (13%)	46 (37%)	**62 (50%)**

Table 3: *Which of the following purposes of analysis are important to your program? Please mark 3—very important, 2—somewhat important, 1—not important*

But the data in Table 4 suggest that this judgment might be too hasty, since 57% of first-year programs still teach students how to analyze imaginative literature (i.e., fiction, drama, or poetry). The most popular kind of text in our sample, taught by 89% of our respondents, was the ubiquitous "essay," that tried-and-true artifact of cultural observation presented to students in gargantuan anthologies that preserve E.B. White's writing like amber preserves ancient bugs. (As of 1999, "Once More to the Lake" showed up in at least 40 anthologies, coming in second to George Orwell's "The Politics of the English Language," which was in 45. See Bloom 967-8.) The next popular artifact for analysis is the "media" text such as film, advertisements, and television shows: 74% of writing programs assign some kind of media artifact for students to analyze. With sources like AmericanRhetoric. com, it is not surprising that 68% of our respondents have students analyze speeches, most likely political speeches that represent the deliberative and epideictic tradition of oratory that has flourished from the founding to the inauguration of Barack Obama. Additionally, at least 54% of us assign students to analyze digital media like Web sites or blogs, suggesting trends toward new media writing (see Wysocki, Johnson-Eilola, Selfe and Sirc).

Essays (e.g., literary journalism, nonfiction prose, public arguments, "Once More to the Lake" by E.B.White)	89%
Film or other forms of mass media (e.g., film, music, advertisements, TV)	74%
Speeches (e.g., Martin Luther King's "I Have a Dream" speech)	68%
Imaginative literature (e.g., fiction, drama, poetry)	57%
Digital media (e.g., Web pages, digital video)	54%
Other	24%

Table 4: *What artifacts or texts does your program assign first-year writing students to analyze? Mark all that apply.*

When it comes to the hermeneutical toolbox we present to students, rhetorical terms are favored over literary ones, though the distinction may not be completely helpful. 85% of our respondents "always" or "frequently" teach terms from informal logic like fallacies, claims, reasons, or induction, and 71% "always" or "frequently" teach classical rhetorical terms like ethos, pathos, and logos, while only 51% "always" or "frequently" teach literary terms like metaphor or diction (see Table 5). Of course, many of us would argue that metaphor and diction are rhetorical terms, but the teachers and administrators in our sample clearly favor approaches to analysis falling in Fulkerson's "procedural rhetoric" category, with a strong leaning toward the tools of argumentation (Fulkerson 671).

What does this survey tell us? Though I cannot generalize with complete confidence, this survey is highly suggestive of how analysis pervades our first-year curriculum. It is widely taught, even more so than research writing or opinion writing. (75% of programs teach the opinion editorial, even though some writers like Patricia Roberts-Miller oppose it.) When asked how many times they assign analysis, administrators and instructors gave us numbers ranging from 2 to 10. One respondent wrote that most writing projects assigned are "rooted" in analysis. Another respondent took issue with the suggestion that analysis is an assignment or "paper," since it smacked of "the old 'modes' approach" that ignored the fact that all writing, according to this respondent, had an analytical component. "I don't see analysis as a genre," wrote another. "It's a tool, a cognitive move, a way of reading critically." And yet it continues to be the most popular writing task in first-year writing, with classical rhetoric and argumentation the most popular theoretical approaches. That more literary approaches, with more literary texts as artifacts, are less frequent is indicative of the enduring control of writing programs by those trained in or informed by rhetoric and composition. Furthermore, we tend to see analysis as a way of helping students evaluate the strength of an argument as it is situated in a rhetorical context of time, audience, and purpose—qualities not as apparent in more literary texts.

Analytical Tool	Never	Occasionally	Frequently	Always
Literary or stylistic terms (e.g., metaphor, voice, diction)	12 (10%)	**50 (40%)**	41 (33%)	22 (18%)
Classical rhetorical terms (e.g., ethos, pathos, logos, kairos, stasis)	4 (3%)	33 (26%)	36 (29%)	**52 (42%)**
Informal logic terms (e.g., claims and reasons, assumptions, logical fallacies, warrants, induction/ deduction)	2 (2%)	16 (13%)	44 (35%)	**63 (50%)**

Table 5: *What analytical terms or tools most frequently are taught to first-year students in your program? Please mark 4—always, 3—frequently, 2—occasionally, and 1—never.*

IV. Can We Teach the Analytical Life?

The answer, I propose, is a qualified *yes*.

I have described what I believe is the lay of the land as far as curriculum goes. I now turn to purpose. Surely we do not teach this kind of writing for its own sake. We believe, or at least our practices lead me to believe we believe, that analytical skill is portable, that its methods go with students to new situations that require analytical reasoning. If it doesn't, then the widespread practice of teaching analysis in a general writing course is suspect. Any discussion of analysis must take into account the contentious issue of *transfer*—whether the skills students learn in general writing courses go with them to different settings, different contexts (see Petraglia). It is not an easy issue, and, in fact, any conclusion that can be drawn from it, including mine, likely will be provisional without further research. Yet considering the assumptions the survey revealed, we must confront the transfer issue or admit that we teach analysis as a ritual act of faith borne of the sweet whisperings of our intuition. If we want to teach for the analytical life, we must be more attentive to the general principles we want our students to abstract from their analyses. It is not sufficient to say that *any* analytical activity will prepare students for *any other*. To ensure our students take analytical skills with them at the end of the semester, we must simplify the task we assign and teach deliberately for transfer.

Put simply, all learning implies transfer—the ability to take knowledge or a skill from one setting and apply it to another setting. In fact "the ultimate goal of schooling," according to the National Research Council, "is to help students transfer what they have learned in school to everyday settings of home, community, and workplace" (73). Seen from one perspective, transfer is not a controversial concept. For example, after we learn to read Dr. Seuss as children, with some degree of success we can read comic books, the back of cereal boxes, or the jokes on the inside of a Laffy Taffy wrapper (see Perkins and Salomon). On the other hand, as two cognitive psychologists put it, "there is little agreement in the scholarly community about the nature of transfer, the extent to which it occurs, and the nature of its underlying mechanisms" (Barnett & Ceci qtd. in Lobato 431). *That* it happens is uncontested; *how* it happens is mysterious, and one hundred years of experimental research has yielded conflicting frameworks and conclusions that suggest—to put it blandly and anticlimactically—the need for further study.

Working either with this literature or independent of it, some composition scholars have concluded that teaching students transferrable skills (like analysis) in first-year writing is a lost cause, and their perceptive and sophisticated critique still stands as an open challenge to our widespread practice of teaching analytical writing in FYC (see Beaufort; Freedman; Petraglia; Russell; Smit). Though their methodologies may differ, their assumptions and conclusions are similar. All cast doubt on the efficacy of what Petraglia calls "general writing skills instruction" (GWSI), the kind of instruction that goes on in the first year, of which analysis is a part. GWSI, according to Petraglia, "has more to do with 'doing school' than it does with teaching students to perform rhetorical tasks" (89). First-year students have "little or no intrinsic motivation to act as rhetors," and their audiences—mainly *us*, let's concede the point—are more intent on "evaluating" rather than understanding or using the writing (91). This was not an original critique when it came out in 1995, but it is a powerful and enduring critique that challenges FYC teachers to account for the genres they assign, especially analysis, the Spam of academic writing. (Would the "research paper," then, be the bologna?)

In separate chapters in the provocative book *Reconceiving Writing, Rethinking Writing Instruction*, published in 1995, Aviva Freedman and David Russell set up the theory behind the critique, echoed recently in works by Beaufort and Smit. Citing genre theorists, language-learning research, and some cognitive psychology, Freedman argues that we learn to write like we learn to speak—in rich social contexts "in response to a rhetorical exigence" (128). From fifteen years of research on Canadian students from elementary school to college, Freedman concludes that comp classrooms lack "the richly elaborated discursive context" of classes in the disciplines, where students pick up the ambience of discourse because the "what, where, when, how, and even why of writing" is more clearly articulated (136-7). Similarly, Russell leans on the work of Vygotsky and activity theory to argue for the apprenticeship model of learning to write. Since "writing does not exist apart from its uses" in a reticulate activity system, first-year writing instruction, insofar as it commits to teaching general writing skills, teaches very little (57). The kind of writing students perform when they analyze exists "for no particular activity system" beyond the classroom (57). Beaufort points out that without a specific discourse community in which to operate, students likely will not see writing assignments like analysis as "authentic" (54). This is what Smit means when he calls analysis a "school genre" (165) that depends on explicit instruction in an artificial environment for an artificial purpose for an artificial audience that, ostensibly, would be interested in reading an analysis of "Once More to the Lake." It is difficult, indeed, to imagine anyone interested in that kind of analysis. (White himself, were he not dead, might gag at the prospect.) My guess is that many teachers, even at their most charitable, find this kind of writing less interesting than other kinds, or maybe any other kind.

Genre theorists have sought to overcome the transfer problem by making analysis a *metacritical* activity that has less to do with what texts say and more with what they *do*. Bawarshi (see also Devitt, Reiff, and Bawarshi) makes *genre analyses*—collecting texts in recurring rhetorical situations (like obituaries), examining the situations in which these texts are embedded, noticing textual regularities and irregularities, and analyzing in writing how text and context interact to create meaning—central to first-year writing (see Bawarshi 158). In *Genre and the Invention of the Writer*, Bawarshi argues that the actual genres first-year writers write are, to a degree, immaterial (168). The goal is to develop a transferrable skill, a content-less rhetorical literacy, that will go with the student to future situations that require genre writing in professional and public life. This argument concedes a point to the critics of FYC mentioned earlier: It seems we cannot truly teach genres outside the contexts in which students will write them.

Then again, Beaufort's study of "Tim," the would-be engineer-writer, strongly suggests that students don't *really* gain specialized rhetorical prowess in a field until they are writing on the job. In the end, it seems the genres do not transfer as well as we hope; we aim, rather, to teach students transferrable rhetorical principles that can be applied "to new situations" beyond FYC (Beaufort 151). "Rather than being artificial genres serving only composition courses," argues Devitt,

> the genres students acquire in our writing classes serve as antecedent genres when students move into other contexts—into discipline-specific courses, into workplaces, and into civic lives. If we ask students to write analytic essays in first-year composition, that genre will be available for them to draw from when they need to write a causal analysis in their history class, a report at work, or a letter to the editor. (204)

Of course the challenge for us is to articulate what analysis looks like as an antecedent genre, since the kind of analysis one does as a historian and the kind one does working for Hewlett-Packard will be very different. Yet as Lee Ann Carroll's research has confirmed, analysis is an appropriate "literacy task" to teach students in the first year of college to prepare them for future tasks in their disciplines and beyond (Carroll 129-30).

One way to make analysis a more useful and transferrable antecedent genre is to make it more an exercise of *situated evaluation* than interpretation. By situated evaluation I mean asking students to evaluate the relative merits of a text for a specific purpose in a specific situation directly related to the students' lives. To carry this point further, it will be useful to contrast what I am proposing with a common first-year genre: rhetorical analysis.

Analysis, indeed, has many instantiations, but one of the prevailing forms champions the *how* of texts over the *what* or the *so what*. As Bazerman and Prior explain, analysis tends to "focus on *what texts do* and *how texts mean* rather than *what they mean*" (3). They argue that students cannot interpret texts in this way unless they overcome their "natural" inclination to ask "what things mean" and start asking "what they do and how they mean" (8). Rhetorical analysis, assigned by 51% of our survey group, is one such assignment that asks students to analyze how a text works in a particular situation for a particular audience that the student may or may not belong to. The standard model was pioneered by Herbert Wichelns, a speech critic at Cornell University in the early twentieth century. Before Wichelns, speech teachers taught speeches in the same way that writing teachers taught essays—as exemplary models to be imitated rather than interpreted (Medhurst xiv). In an article published in 1925, Wichelns argued that rhetorical analysis "is concerned with effect" and "regards a speech as a communication to a specific audience, and holds its business to be the analysis and appreciation for the orator's method of imparting his ideas to his hearers," i.e., the hearers at the particular historical moment (26).

Rhetorical analysis requires the student to know something of the speaker and the situation, the intended audience and purpose, the main argument and the supporting evidence, the arrangement and style, and, most importantly, the "effect of the discourse on its immediate hearers," which, in some instances, could be determined by studying news accounts of the speech event (29). Though speech communication scholars have moved far beyond this model in their discussion of criticism, English rhetoricians—especially those responsible for writing programs—have continued to define rhetorical analysis in pretty much the same way Wichelns did. For example, Jack Selzer defines rhetorical analysis as "an effort to understand how people within specific social situations attempt to influence others through language" (281). Similarly, for Fahnestock and Secor, rhetorical analysis (1) "pays attention to the who, when, where, and probably why of a text;" (2) "uses an identifiable vocabulary drawn from the rhetorical tradition," which includes Aristotelian terms like *ethos, pathos,* and *logos*; (3) "identifies language choices that serve the rhetor's ostensible purpose;" and (4) "seeks to uncover the argument of a text" (182-4).

On its face this kind of assignment seems incredibly valuable. It teaches students to look for the strategies writers, speakers, and performers use to persuade, convince, and move us. Yet a fundamental ambiguity exists that keeps us from making this kind of analysis as useful as it could be. A traditional rhetorical analysis in the mode of Wichelns would focus on audience—i.e., the *intended* audience of the artifact being analyzed. Selzer calls this "contextual [rhetorical] analysis" because it takes into account the specific context a text is embedded in. Normally when we read a text, we assume that we are the intended audience. But when we "read rhetorically" we essentially eavesdrop "on what someone is saying or writing to someone else," and we "may or may not care much about the issue" (Selzer 282). "As a rhetorical analyst," Selzer continues, "your job is not so much to react to these rhetorical acts as understand them better, to appreciate the rhetorical situation" (282). Leff and Mohrmann's reading of Lincoln's Cooper Union speech is a model of this kind of analysis, the kind that takes into account "the immediate rhetorical motives" behind the speech and its immediate audience of Northern Republicans on the eve of the Civil War (358).

This kind of assignment asks students to disengage themselves from the text, assume a position of critical distance, and then make analytical assumptions about how a text might be received based on what is understood of the original purpose and intended audience. To perform this analysis, students make assumptions about why a text would be persuasive for an intended audience, and by so doing they commit what Steve Fuller calls an act of "humanist hubris" (292) by assuming that unknown, and reductively understood, audiences receive texts in the same way rhetorical critics do, and that audiences are consciously persuaded by the same "specter of hidden tropes" that rhetorical critics conjure up in their analyses (294). This critique of rhetorical analysis might be too dismissive; there is evident value in getting students to think creatively about how texts work in rich contexts for various audiences. But there may be a better way to engage students in the practice of rhetorical criticism, without leading them to make guesses about how Martin Luther King's rhetoric would be received by his immediate historical audience in 1963 America. And there is a better way to ensure that students transfer their analytical abilities to other settings where the texts they encounter will not be as aesthetically rich.

I have been teaching rhetorical analysis for almost a decade and have been unhappy with the writing my students do. This, to me, is a sure sign that there is something wrong with my assignment and not my students. "My" assignment, however, is not really mine—rhetorical analysis is part of the bread and butter of a dozen textbooks and (I imagine) hundreds of programs in the comp world. To teach it, we give students articles frozen in time (like FDR's speech after the Pearl Harbor attack) and introduce them to a forest of rhetorical terms they must first internalize and then use to analyze the texts they read. Sometimes (at least 68% of the time, according to our survey) these historical speeches make it impossible for students to do anything but appreciate the greatness of the good man speaking well. It shocks no one when a new semester of students finds the "I Have a Dream" speech eloquent and persuasive. When they write this kind of analysis, they plow over a plowed field as analytical observers whose critical faculties have been circumscribed. Students interpret not as contemporaries of King in a critical moment of public debate, but as necessarily awed appreciators of someone's already established rhetorical skill. And even if they are assigned the task of evaluating the merits of a less-regarded argument, they do so outside the transaction, making somewhat reductive, and often painfully obvious, observations about how this ad or this speech or this essay persuades a target audience to which they do not necessarily belong.

Such approaches could, in fact, be useful to teach the "rhetoricality" of text in general, which Petraglia argues is all we can expect to transfer out of first-year writing (95). But I believe we must do more, or maybe less. If we can teach students to *evaluate* rather than just *interpret* an argument, we will teach them to be citizen-critics engaging in public debate over the merits of arguments about issues that influence us all. I argue that one problem with rhetorical analysis, as often taught, is that it focuses on "the efficacy of devices" rather than "the validity of arguments" (Fuller 294). In other words, it teaches students to appreciate or analyze how an apt metaphor works without asking them whether it *should* work, a question that brings both student and text into a live milieu of public debate—the kind of debate that matters right now. The word "critic," as Noel Carroll points out in *On Criticism*, implies someone who makes judgments about the value of something and whose appraisal is itself argumentative. The critic occupies a "social role" in that he or she helps an audience understand the value of a text and form judgments of their own (Carroll 45). In this role, students seek to convince other members of protopublics and publics to be or not to be convinced by arguments meant to change the course of public attitude and behavior.

Situated evaluation treats texts as live missives in public conversations in the reticulate publics students inhabit. Gerard Hauser defines a public—small "p"—as "a discursive space in which individuals and groups associate to discuss matters of mutual interest and, where possible, to reach a common judgment about them" (61). These spaces emerge from the back and forthness of a rhetoric whose *telos* is practical judgment—the kind that helps us know how to feel, think, and act in the context of public controversy. From this perspective, an invitation to analyze is an invitation to act as *judge*, as a citizen among citizens; an invitation to *write* analysis, even in a situation as cloistered and seemingly removed as a first-year comp class, is an invitation to argue about the value of "actually occurring discourse" to help shape common judgment (Hauser 273).

This kind of orientation to a text is normative in the sense that students use the tools of critical thinking to exercise judgment about the relative merits of an argument. Scholars of critical thinking divide the cognitive task of analysis into two main parts: *identifying* an argument (i.e., deciding the argument's claims, reasons, assumptions, and conclusions) and *evaluating* an argument (i.e., testing assumptions, ambiguities, or omissions) to determine whether it is convincing (see Dick; Ennis; Fisher). Unlike the standard rhetorical analysis of "Once More to the Lake" that determines its already over-determined strategies, this kind of evaluative critical thinking has a direct influence on the lives of our students since it helps them conclude "what to believe or what to do in a given context" (Giancarlo and Facione 30). Students use what Hauser calls "local norms of reasonableness" to help others evaluate arguments in the deliberative sphere they belong to (61). And of course a student's analysis is itself argumentative, as are the norms they use to evaluate a text.

Unlike other forms of analysis, this approach has been shown to transfer to other domains in research studies. In an article in *American Psychologist* that summarizes the research, Diane Halpern describes critical thinking as "the purposeful, reasoned, and goal-directed" process "involved in solving problems, formulating inferences, calculating likelihoods, and making decisions" (450-1). It is a "higher-order cognitive skill," as the NSSE report argues, but it should also be taught as a metacognitive activity that is "reflective, sensitive to the context, and self-monitored" (Halpern 451). If students are taught analysis explicitly and deliberately as a transferrable skill, they will be more prepared in future experiences to activate the steps of critical analysis. Such "focusing phenomena," as Lobato calls them, "regularly direct students' attention toward certain properties or patterns" they will encounter later (442). If we can make the properties and patterns of analysis far more simple than we have in the past, students will leave our classrooms prepared to analyze arguments in other settings.

This last semester my students and I met one morning to talk about Facebook—more specifically, to talk about an article in the student newspaper about Facebook. A student-journalist had written a trenchant critique of the online social networking site, and I wanted to know whether my students accepted the critique. We looked at the reasons, lined up like soldiers with weapons drawn. The writer argued that Facebook led students to withdraw from "authentic" relationships, that it could be addictive, that it celebrated superficial friendships, and invited dissemblance—all commonplaces about social networking sites. Some of the students were convinced; some weren't. The conversation, though, turned into a debate about the unwritten assumptions (called warrants by Toulmin) that tied the assertions together. One student concluded that if Facebook was inauthentic, then phone conversations were as well. Another pointed out that the critique against adding acquaintances to your profile assumed no possible benefits for doing so. Ultimately my students were trying to convince each other to accept or reject an argument meant for them, in their rhetorical situation, with *kairotic* importance for their lives now lived.

The analytical life I imagine for my students begins with the deliberative discourse students inhabit as citizens and group members. Instead of analyzing John Muir's "Save the Hetch-Hetchy Valley," a fine essay that could be usefully assigned for other tasks, students should analyze the latest political discourse on health care or their college's policies. As citizen critics, they need to know how to *identify* and *evaluate* salient vernacular arguments whose authors want students to think or act in certain ways, to vote and consume in certain ways, to be *subjected* to power dynamics in certain ways (see Hauser). By reframing analysis as an act of critical evaluation, we not only loose ourselves from the power of the commercially-packaged readers, we teach, in the words of John Dewey, "critical sense and methods of discriminating judgment" that makes coordinated political action possible (*Later Works* 337). In addition, if we reframe the assignment as a public act of evaluation, we give our students a rich rhetorical situation to inhabit analogous to the deliberation about the Constitution and other public disagreements that require rhetorical analysis, the antecedent genre of critical democracy.

Acknowledgements

I thank my research assistants, Ty Campbell and Jalena Reschke, the audience at the 2009 Rocky Mountain Modern Language Association Conference, and the anonymous reviewers and editorial staff at *Composition Studies* for their contributions to this article.

Works Cited

Adler, Mortimer, and Charles van Doren. *How to Read a Book*. New York: Touchstone, 1972. Print.

Bawarshi, Anis. *Genre and the Invention of the Writer: Reconsidering the Place of Invention in Composition*. Logan: Utah State UP, 2003. Print.

Bazerman, Charles, and Paul Prior. Introduction. *What Writing Does and How it Does It: An Introduction to Analyzing Texts and Textual Practices*. Ed. Charles Bazerman and Paul Prior. Mahwah: Lawrence Erlbaum, 2004. 1-10. Print.

Beaufort, Anne. *College Writing and Beyond: A New Framework for University Writing Instruction*. Logan: Utah State UP, 2007. Print.

Bloom, Lynn Z. "The Essay Canon." *The Norton Book of Composition Studies*. Ed. Susan Miller. New York: Norton, 2009. 945-72. Print.

Brereton, John C., ed. *The Origins of Composition Studies in the American College, 1875-1925: A Documentary History*. Pittsburgh: U of Pittsburgh P, 1995. Print.

Carroll, Lee Ann. *Rehearsing New Roles: How College Students Develop as Writers*. Carbondale: Southern Illinois UP, 2002. Print.

Carroll, Noel. *On Criticism*. New York: Routledge, 2009. Print.

Clark, Donald Lemen. *Rhetoric in Greco-Roman Education*. New York: Columbia UP, 1957. Print.

Devitt, Amy. *Writing Genres*. Carbondale: Southern Illinois UP, 2004. Print.

Devitt, Amy, Mary Jo Reiff, and Anis Bawarshi. *Scenes of Writing: Strategies for Composing with Genres*. New York: Longman, 2004. Print.

Dewey, John. *The Early Works, 1882-1898*. Ed. Jo Ann Boydston. Carbondale: Southern Illinois UP, 1972. Print. Vol. 5 of *The Collected Works of John Dewey*. 37 vols. 1967-87.

———. *The Later Works, 1925-1953*. Ed. Jo Ann Boydston. Carbondale: Southern Illinois UP, 1984. Print. Vol. 2 of *The Collected Works of John Dewey*. 37 vols. 1967-1987.

Dick, R. Dale. "An Empirical Taxonomy of Critical Thinking." *Journal of Instructional Psychology* 18.2 (1991): 79-92. Print.

Ennis, Robert H. "A Concept of Critical Thinking." *Harvard Educational Review* 32.1 (Winter 1962): 81-111. Print.

Fahnestock, Jeanne, and Marie Secor. "Rhetorical Analysis." *Discourse Studies in Composition*. Ed. Ellen Barton and Gail Stygall. Cresskill: Hampton, 2002. 177-200. Print.

Fisher, Alec. *Critical Thinking: An Introduction*. Cambridge: Cambridge UP, 2001. Print.

Freedman, Aviva. "The What, Where, When, Why, and How of Classroom Genres." *Reconceiving Writing, Rethinking Writing Instruction*. Ed. Joseph Petraglia. Mahwah: Lawrence Erlbaum, 1995. 121-44. Print.

Fulkerson, Richard. "Composition at the Turn of the Twenty-First Century." *CCC* 56.4 (2005): 654-87. Print.

Fuller, Steve. "'Rhetoric of Science': Double the Trouble?" *Rhetorical Hermeneutics: Invention and Interpretation in the Age of Science*. Ed. Alan G. Gross and William M. Keith. Albany: SUNY P, 1997. 279-98. Print.

Genung, John Franklin. *Handbook of Rhetorical Analysis: Studies in Style and Invention*. Boston: Ginn & Co, 1888. Print.

Giancarlo, Carol Ann, and Peter A. Facione. "A Look Across Four Years at the Disposition Toward Critical Thinking Among Undergraduate Students." *The Journal of General Education* 50.1 (2001): 29-55. Print.

Graff, Gerald. *Clueless in Academe: How Schooling Obscures the Life of the Mind*. New Haven: Yale, 2003. Print.

———. *Professing Literature: An Institutional History*. Chicago: U of Chicago P, 1987. Print.

Gross, Alan G., and William M. Keith. *Rhetorical Hermeneutics: Invention and Interpretation in the Age of Science*. Albany: SUNY P, 1997. Print.

Halpern, Diane F. "Teaching Critical Thinking for Transfer Across Domains." *American Psychologist* 53.4 (April 1998): 449-55. Print.

Hauser, Gerard. *Vernacular Voices: The Rhetoric of Publics and Public Spheres*. Columbia: U of South Carolina P, 1999. Print.

Hillocks, George. *Research on Written Composition*. Urbana: NCTE, 1986. Print.

Huber, Bettina. "Undergraduate English Programs: Findings from an MLA Survey of the 1991-92 Academic Year." *ADE Bulletin* 115 (Winter 1996): 34-73. Print.

Jackson, Brian. "Cultivating Paideweyan Pedagogy: Rhetoric Education in English and Communication Studies." *Rhetoric Society Quarterly* 37 (2007): 181-201. Print.

Kress, Gunther, and Theo van Leeuwen. *Reading Images: The Grammar of Visual Design*. 2nd ed. London: Routledge, 2006. Print.

Leff, Michael C., and Gerald P. Mohrmann. "Lincoln at Cooper Union: A Rhetorical Analysis of the Text." *Quarterly Journal of Speech* 60 (1974): 346-58. Print.

Lobato, Joanne. "Alternative Perspectives on the Transfer of Learning: History, Issues, and Challenges for Future Research." *Journal of the Learning Sciences* 15.4 (2006): 431-49. Print.

Medhurst, Martin J., ed. "The Academic Study of Public Address." *Landmark Essays in American Public Address*. Davis: Hermagoras, 1993. xi-xliii. Print.

National Research Council. *How People Learn: Brain, Mind, Experience, and School*. Expanded ed. Washington: National Academy, 2000. Print.

Perkins, D.N., and Gavriel Salomon. "Teaching for Transfer." *Educational Leadership* 46.1 (1988): 22-32.

Petraglia, Joseph. "Writing as an Unnatural Act." *Reconceiving Writing, Rethinking Writing Instruction*. Ed. Joseph Petraglia. Mahwah: Lawrence Erlbaum, 1995. 79-100. Print.

"Promoting Engagement for All Students: The Imperative to Look Within." National Survey of Student Engagement. 2008. Web. 4 Nov. 2009.

Pynchon, Thomas. *Gravity's Rainbow*. New York: Penguin, 1995. Print.

Roberts-Miller, Patricia. *Deliberate Conflict: Argument, Political Theory, and Composition Classes*. Carbondale: Southern Illinois UP, 2004. Print.

Russell, David. "Activity Theory and its Implications for Writing Instruction."

Reconceiving Writing, Rethinking Writing Instruction. Ed. Joseph Petraglia. Mahwah: Lawrence Erlbaum, 1995. 51-77. Print.

Selzer, Jack. "Rhetorical Analysis: Understanding How Texts Persuade Readers." *What Writing Does and How It Does It: An Introduction to Analyzing Texts and Textual Practices*. Ed. Charles Bazerman and Paul Prior. Mahwah: Lawrence Erlbaum, 2004. 279-307. Print.

Smit, David. *The End of Composition Studies*. Carbondale: Southern Illinois UP, 2004. Print.

Wardle, Elizabeth. "Understanding 'Transfer' from FYC: Preliminary Results of a Longitudinal Study." *WPA: Writing Program Administration* 31.1-2 (Fall/Winter 2007): 65-85. Print.

Wichelns, Herbert A. "The Literary Criticism of Oratory." *Landmark Essays in American Public Address*. Ed. Martin J. Medhurst. Davis: Hermagoras, 1993. 1-32. Print.

Wysocki, Anne Frances, Johndan Johnson-Eilola, Cynthia L. Selfe, and Geoffrey Sirc, eds. *Writing New Media*. Logan: Utah State UP, 2004. Print.

Writing Beyond Borders: Rethinking the Relationship Between Composition Studies and Professional Writing

Jennifer Bay

This essay attempts to forge connections between the fields of Composition Studies and professional writing. I argue that a stronger relationship would foster more sustainable ties in light of the corporate university and global capitalism. I point to three of what Dale Jacobs calls *threshold spaces*, sites where we can foster a culture of hospitality between professional writing and Composition Studies. These three spaces—emerging technologies, work, and service learning—provide new avenues for thinking about how both professional writing and Composition Studies can foster adaptability within the changing university and the larger world.

Let us say yes to who or what turns up, before any determination, before any anticipation, before any identification, whether or not it has to do with a foreigner, an immigrant, an invited guest, or an unexpected visitor, whether or not the new arrival is a citizen of another country, a human, animal, or divine creature, a living or dead thing, male or female.
—Jacques Derrida, *Of Hospitality* (77)

Cynthia Haynes's Kinneavy award-winning essay, "Writing Offshore: The Disappearing Coastline of Composition Theory," invokes a Derridean call for "forms of solidarity yet to be invented" (705). In reconsidering the state of composition theory, Haynes asks us to move away from the ground on which we have cemented our theories about writing—which Haynes identifies as argument—instead promoting a conception of "writing offshore." Writing offshore would leave behind argument as a grounding theory for composition and teach students to "think *in* the *abstract*, in writing" (677). "Learning to abstract," Haynes explains, "would involve learning the alluring nature of language, how it draws you away, how it seduces you" (715). An offshore approach would force Composition Studies to (re)think itself in sophistic ways, a call that many have made but to which few have responded.[1]

This essay seeks to respond to the call for offshore futures, visions of what Composition Studies might become or invent for itself, by rethinking the relationship between Composition Studies and professional writing.[2] Pursuing such a future would involve moving away from the safe foundation(s) on which Composition Studies is firmly planted, much like it once pushed off from the beaches of current-traditional rhetoric; similarly, professional

Composition Studies 38.2 (2010): 29-46

writing would need to do the same, to move out into the open, away from the safely built shorelines of institution and organization. Abandoning these grounds in favor of movement might forge a new relation between two fields of study that have much more in common than often discussed.

As already noted by professional writing scholars, Composition Studies and professional writing share various commonalities,[3] including a strong rhetorical heritage. But that rhetorical heritage often manifests itself as the ground of argument. Some might argue that reason and argument form the basis of writing in business and industry, and as such, we must teach argumentative logic to our professional writing students.[4] But incidents such as the Enron scandal, the dot com bust, and the Microsoft antitrust case prove that traditional logic does not always hold in professional writing situations; *"so much defies reason"* (Haynes 669). The *Challenger* shuttle disaster is taught and often held as an exemplar of why argument is important to professional writing situations.[5] If those engineers had been more effective communicators, the argument goes—more persuasive—then the accident might have been prevented. But more persuasive doesn't always mean logical or ethical.[6] Similarly, many strands of composition either embrace argument outright, or in various pedagogical modes, and critique culture and capitalism from the same argumentative well. In both instances, argument becomes problem-solving.

What is missing from analyses of such situations is an understanding that the logic driving these professional decisions is not the same logic that grounds traditional argument. It is the logic of advanced multinational capitalism, which is *groundless*. Like the terror cells that currently plague the Western world, capitalism has no terra firma, no physical ground on which it is planted. Neither Composition Studies nor professional writing has fully acknowledged the implications of this understanding in their theories and approaches. We continue to focus on logical argument and traditional rhetorical configurations as the basis of our pedagogies; we try to place the template of reason and logic over images, visual structures, and online publishing.[7] But this logic, as Haynes so eloquently writes, does not work for the new world order, nor does it always apply to other cultures and countries who may abide by different ways of thinking and living.

While Haynes provides a compelling discussion on deconstructing the ground of argument, in this essay I turn to a related type of ground that requires reconsideration: the border that separates professional writing and Composition Studies. Both Composition Studies and professional writing have tried to forge separate disciplinary identities, but I believe that the creation of a different sort of solidarity between these two areas might allow rhetoric and writing to gain elevated status in the university and in the culture at large. This solidarity is not something that can be easily outlined or modeled, but like Derrida's approach in *Of Hospitality*, let us say *yes* to what shows up, say *yes* to all possibilities before we become engulfed in the moment of (self) identification as other. A hospitable *yes* would welcome new ways of thinking about rhetoric, as well as emerging forms of writing. This sense of hospitality might allow us to nurture and sustain the delicate links between humanistic and technological inquiries that are inherent to both fields of study.

Composition has recently turned to the concept of hospitality as a way of rethinking the relationship between student and teacher in the classroom and between professionals in the university. Janice Haswell, Richard Haswell, and Glenn Blalock, for instance, present three different modes of hospitality and privilege a sense of transformative hospitality to the writing classroom. Dale Jacobs promotes a monastic hospitality, "radical in its acceptance of all, including those who might be hostile to us" (566). Jacobs proposes the deployment of hospitality in our professional lives and in our interactions with others; such hospitality, he argues, would open us up to the possibility of transformation (564). We might extend this application to the disciplinary grounds on which the university is built, grounds that are already shifting with budget crises and the focus on interdisciplinary and global collaborations. A form of solidarity between professional writing and Composition Studies would also necessitate the abandonment of grounds and borders that tie us to outmoded understandings of writing and thinking in favor of a new and mutual hospitality.

More practically, Composition Studies and professional writing each possess strengths from which the other can benefit. The global and technological landscape of our world necessitates that students share both a critical understanding of advanced capitalism as well as an understanding of advanced writing technologies. Conversations on the global economy are happening in both fields, but are rarely referenced across disciplines. Likewise, professional writing's attention to advanced writing technologies in the workplace, especially multimedia and digital production processes, can facilitate the development and full integration of digital composition in the university.

In the remainder of this essay, I discuss the current shifting climate of the university to demonstrate that first, the ground is already shifting, which might be articulated through the emergence of network logic and creative thinking, and that second, a solidarity among writing studies, broadly conceived, is a first step toward working against an academic climate which fosters uncritical problem-solving. I then point to three of what Dale Jacobs calls *threshold spaces*, sites where we can foster a culture of hospitality between professional writing and Composition Studies. These three spaces—emerging technologies, work, and service learning—provide new avenues for thinking about how both professional writing and Composition Studies can foster adaptability within the changing university and the larger world.

Collapsing the Logic of Borders

Research on borders, borderlands, and contact zones proliferated in the 1990s. Fueled by multiculturalism, gender studies, and accelerating globalization, the metaphor of the border served as a rich symbol of the ways academics might account for various forms of difference and for other groups within and beyond the university. But as Daniel Mahala and Jody Swilky observe, while "reform discourse is often full of geographically-inflected language rallying us to negotiate the 'contact zone,' 'redraw the boundaries,' 'cross borders,' 'break down the walls of the university,'" there is little attention paid to "the issue of power geometry" (766-7). Power geometries refer to "the different ways in which groups and individuals are *inserted into* time and space, helped or hurt by the ways it is constantly being reconfigured" (766). Global capitalism imperiously reconfigures the time and spacing of groups. We see this in the current economic situation, where outsourcing, unemployment, reduced wages and benefits, and the erosion of pensions and social security have affected students and workers, both in the U.S. and abroad. Shifting economic realities show us that there is no ground on which we can rely. *"We are all boat people,"* as Haynes observes (697). Look around and we see more change than stability: students change majors multiple times based on job possibilities; faculty spend years searching for full-time employment and often must pursue other careers due to the lack of positions; workers make career changes or return to school for job training and ensured future income; and elderly retirees must work to supplement their subsidized incomes. These are just a few images of the constantly shifting landscape on which Composition Studies attempts to build its constituency.

Mahala and Swilky attempt to outline a deeper understanding of how "disciplinary knowledge functions in relation to built environments and the social and economic forces that assemble, delimit, and circulate people in them" (767). If we approach the situation from their perspective, the key problem, then, is not simply change—that change is happening all around or that we even need to change. Rather, there is an emerging tension between the kinds of change contemporary capitalism drives and our attempts to grapple with it. Thus, our attempts to change will fall flat to the extent that they remain grounded in old methods and disciplinary identities. As Mahala and Swilky explain, "while humanities faculty in all sort of institutions battle over multiculturalism and critical methods, the ground on which we stand is literally changing beneath our feet, and our standard ways of framing disciplinary issues and problems are ill-equipped to address the new conditions" (777). We need a new way of making sense of this constantly shifting ground, but as Haynes demonstrates, it can't be the ground of argument, and I would go further to say that it also can't be the ground of disciplinarity.

The ground—both physical and rhetorical—has always been and is always changing. Sometimes that shifting ground is not visible to us because of physical locations or mental limitations. We are (always already) groundless. The more we try to ground our pedagogies and theories of rhetoric and writing, the more we eclipse the possible connections that can allow us to navigate those shifting grounds.

This lack of grounding pervades every aspect of the university environment, from disciplinary structures to individuals and even to points within our own fields. The definitional debates, such as what defines professional writing or what defines academic writing, are only one telling example. In professional writing, this debate has played out through the proper name. What do we call this field: technical writing, business writing, professional writing, technical communication? Jo Allen points out the benefits of not naming the field, allowing its fluidity and adaptability to become its strengths ("Case" 76). We see this in Composition Studies through a more fluid understanding of what comprises writing. Kathleen Blake Yancey, among others, was one of the first to attempt to move toward an understanding that new technologies change what we mean by composing or writing, creating a broader and differently inflected sense of what we mean by composition.[8]

But a more important point for this discussion is that emerging writing technologies are collapsing two formerly clear delineations that were often used to separate composition from professional writing: the lines between academic and nonacademic writing and the distinction between professional and amateur. Digital rhetoric, for instance, has attained prominence not only because of the proliferation of images, video, and multimedia in Western culture, but also because *computer software allows almost anyone with access to create those same types of images, video, and multimedia*. The Internet allows anyone to invent, to publish, regardless of whether they are "professionals" or not. What it means to be a "professional," then, is changing with new forms of personal publishing. Weblogs, wikis, and Web site development, for instance, allow anyone to publish and edit content online. Journalists such as Dan Gillmor have lauded the development of "participatory media," in which citizens can become journalists. In professional contexts, downsizing and budget cuts allow companies to seize the potential of new technologies. Rather than relying solely on technical support personnel and print manuals, companies are creating user forums for their products, where users take responsibility for sharing information, help, and support. User manuals are being published solely online in .pdf,

.xml, or .html form. Moreover, users are creating their own support communities online to solve problems and share information formerly reserved for "experts."

And personal publishing allows anyone to not only publish but also allows for corporate sponsorship and support of Web sites. Movie and television outlets, for instance, are finding that personal and collaborative fan Web sites are a great advertising resource, not to mention a burgeoning market of consumers. Among all of these developments, our students become more savvy and knowledgeable about new media composition through outside of class applications of Photoshop, Flash, and other Web development tools. What does it mean that our first-year composition students, then, can create and operate their own sophisticated Web sites and *make money from them* through Google AdSense, corporate sponsorship, or donations? The surge of interest in entrepreneurial education is evidence of the following fact: we've not only shifted to the student as consumer; we've also shifted to the student as producer of capital. Unfortunately, the reality is that most students do not engage in this digital capital as much as low-wage toil in order to support themselves. Composition, for instance, grounded in a sense of academic preparation through thesis-driven, problem-solving argument, is not just ill-equipped to genuinely and pervasively help students here; it does not even understand how to field, much less actively pursue, the question.

If the university, as Bill Readings, Stanley Aronowitz, and others have argued, is governed by corporate logic and if students are consumers, then what we call "academic writing" is already inflected by this corporate logic and can no longer be seen as necessarily distinct from nonacademic writing. Aronowitz describes the current academic system as blurring boundaries between what he sees as originally separate concepts: "The current academic system has fudged the distinctions between training, education, and learning" (158). The university "is caught in a market logic that demands students be job-ready upon graduation" (158). But as Royer and Gilles remind us in their discussion of creating a writing department, there has always been blurring between these concepts for rhetoricians (32). Rhetoric in the nineteenth century, for instance, was a practical or applied art in which individuals learned rhetoric to train for jobs upon graduation.

We can see this among faculty ranks with the renewed interest in the public intellectual. Cornell West, Stanley Fish, and Michael Bérubé have migrated from writing only for academic venues to composing for broader audiences in the hopes of creating a greater influence for their ideas. In this way, they have become public commentators on politics and social concerns. Their writing is no longer limited to scholarly articles, books, and publications, which are themselves immersed in the crisis that is academic publishing. They have moved to more popular and accessible venues such as mainstream books, magazines, blogs, and online forums.

Other scholars have attained prominence—and even jobs—through sites such as Twitter.[9] The expansion of possible audiences indicates that the boundaries of what qualifies as academic writing are changing and thus are not so easily defined.

Nevertheless, controversy such as the reprimands leveled at West for neglecting the academic as he sought a more popular presence indicate to what extent shifts in what we call "academic writing" continually bump up against entrenched disciplinary attitudes about what constitutes writing in a specific area. We need new ways of thinking about the technologies and economic realities that are shifting how we understand writing in various contexts. The next section attempts to theorize those shifts in terms of the network logic that fuel their circulation and how hospitality between disciplines might work to unhinge the boundaries that separate professional writing and Composition Studies.

New Models for Creative Thinking

In many ways, the blurring of boundaries and the shifting of grounds can be understood through what Mark C. Taylor calls "network culture" in *The Moment of Complexity*. Taylor describes some of the attributes of network culture in which "[e]verything moves faster and faster until speed becomes an end in itself" (3). In network culture, information is no longer mere data; we humans have also become pieces of data: "Many physical, chemical, and biological processes are also information processes. This expanded notion of information makes it necessary to reconfigure the relation between nature and culture in such a way that neither is reduced to the other but that both emerge and coevolve in intricate interrelations" (4). What Taylor makes clear is that it's too easy to position corporate culture against humanistic values (or scientific values against humanism, for that matter). The relationship is more complex than a simple binary; rather, the two are co-adaptive to one another. This combinatory, interactive logic of the network is what now drives industry and the university.

Network theory provides one way to rethink the theories that seem to divide Composition Studies and professional writing. Rather than conceive them as two separate disciplines, we might consider them part of a network of productive processes. Historically, professional writing has oriented itself toward a production model in which there is a "finished" product (usually demanded or required in business and industry). It's also a field in which the writing is always presented as having a "real" audience or "real" function. Composition Studies, on the other hand, orients itself toward process, toward revision, and only recently has responded to the call to produce texts with real-world effects. Even the seemingly briefly-lived interest in post-process theory found its meaning and ground in the process movement. But students don't separate process and product (production and consumption) except according to how teachers present writing to them. Production is a constant process, and students already see this through their own writing, especially on the Web where revision and design are potentially infinite. As Royer and Gilles put it, "an interest in the *production* of texts has been the linchpin of writing studies for many years" (34). Why, then, aren't Composition Studies and professional writing constituting themselves as part of this constant production? One reason may be that these disciplines too often define themselves against each other across a binary division. Professional writing's connection to business and industry creates tensions with Composition Studies, which often aligns itself with cultural and post-Marxist critique. Composition's attachment to academic writing distances it from professional writing's focus on workplace writing situations. Yet Composition's service ethic implicitly elevates other disciplines, hamstringing Composition's potential to re-imagine ways for the academic, the popular, and workplace writing to transform each other; the same might be said for professional writing's service to business and industry.

What we need is more *hospitality* between Composition Studies and professional writing, more attempts to collaborate and realize the productive spaces of the network in which we are enmeshed. Professional writing scholars have already called for more collaboration with other fields. In assessing the state of technical communication research, Ann Blakeslee and Rachel Spilka advise that technical communication "needs to ensure the vitality and quality of [...] the field's relationship with other, related disciplines" (82). They cite Davida Charney's advice against

> separating ourselves too much from other fields, including rhetoric and composition, from which many of us developed the theoretical and pedagogical foundations of our work. According to Charney, there is danger in repeating mistakes of the past by isolating ourselves completely from issues in writing instruction, theory, and scholarship. Because we share many concerns with these colleagues, we stand to experience greater gains than losses from maintaining our connections with them. (85)

The problem with this excellent advice is that it is positioned within an argument for raising the status of the field of technical communication. Alliances with Rhetoric and Composition are not advocated for their inherent worth, for mutual and transformative benefit, but for the state of research in the field. Is this a hospitable approach to a field that shares rhetoric as its "mother tongue"?

The connections that Charney advocates could not operate merely on the surface; they would have to operate at all levels: administration, pedagogy, and theory. Some glimpses of how such an alliance plays out on the administrative level is found in Richard Johnson-Sheehan and Charles Paine's article on collaborative program administration, "Changing the Center of Gravity: Collaborative Writing Program Administration in Large Universities." Johnson-Sheehan and Paine discuss a new collaborative model of WPA work: writing programs that share the administration of a comprehensive rhetoric or writing program among composition and professional writing scholars. They report that in this model, "a cluster of writing programs and courses are subsumed into a single program that is administered by a team of rhetoric scholars" (200). This administrative unification, though, is largely precipitated by what Johnson-Sheehan and Paine call "the material realities of expanding writing programs" (200). While both programs rely on "rhetoric as a mother discipline," the forced unification made obvious that these writing programs were "divided by different cultures and different languages" (200). Johnson-Sheehan and Paine report that composition was largely aligned with a humanities-based culture while professional writing was aligned with scientific-technical culture. But the article only focuses on how administration can be collaborative, not on how one specific knowledge can influence another. The current structure of university is centered on student and economic needs. How can professional writing scholars bring their specific knowledge of workplace cultures to bear on administering a large-scale writing program? Because the university operates on corporate logic, their knowledge of business and industry can be beneficial to writing program administration. In a way, the WPA is the ultimate professional writer. She writes documentation, business correspondence, reports, observations, and performs primary research often using human subjects. Trying out a new assignment or pedagogical technique is a type of usability testing she undertakes. Similarly, composition scholars can help professional writing not seem so needs-driven; there is the potential to see new ways of seeing the work of first-year writing that values language in its multiplicity and not solely to solve a problem.[10]

Pedagogically, solidarity between the two areas can assist with instructional goals, especially integrating writing technologies into the curriculum. Professional writing's focus on writing technologies can be brought to bear on first-year writing courses which, because of their size and number, have greater difficulty fully integrating technology into the curriculum. An alliance with professional writing might also allow for corporate or industry funding for Composition Studies. Or better yet, composition courses might become an experimental environment where software developers can "try out" or test their developing products on a future population. Rather than professional writing courses, which generally contain upper-level students in business and technology majors, composition courses would provide a wide variety of students with various backgrounds and proficiencies. Part of the class assignments could be inventive: What can you see yourself using this product for and why? How are you actually using the tool? Students could figure out creative ways to use developing products and write (about) those creative uses.

Similarly, the critique of industry and culture common in first-year composition can be brought to bear on professional writing courses. While there has been an attention to cultural studies critiques in professional writing, it's not always clear how those critiques are brought to bear on professional writing classrooms in which students are subject to workplace interests. We see plenty of workplace studies that use cultural studies methodologies and approaches, but practical classroom assignments and activities are less common, unless they are connected with ethics. As Thomas Frank so clearly, yet cynically elaborates, "Yes, career-minded students are still interested in deep understandings of fan communities and audience 'resistance,' but not so much to celebrate these things as to learn how to work with them or around them" (52). Cultural studies analyses, then, can prove useful for professional writing students who can inspect the crevices of corporate culture and use that future knowledge in creative ways. Indeed, it is this creativity that corporate culture desires most in college graduates. After all, America's greatest product is culture (Frank 33).

Another way to align the pedagogical goals between these two fields could be through abstract, or what might be called creative, thinking. Creative thinking is the key point that fuels Richard Florida's characterization of the "creative class." As Florida notes in his book, *The Rise of the Creative Class*, the newly emergent social class is the "creative class," which includes writers, artists, designers, engineers, and anyone who uses creativity in their professional work. People in this creative class, Florida explains, "share a common creative ethos that values creativity, individuality, difference, and merit. For members of the Creative Class, every aspect and every manifestation of creativity—technological, cultural, and economic—is interlinked and inseparable" (8). He estimates that as much as a third of the American workforce and at least a quarter of the European workforce are members of this creative class (xiv). Florida goes on to contend that creativity is and always has been essential to the ways that we live and work, "involving distinct kinds of thinking and habits that must be cultivated both in the individual and in the surrounding society" (21-2). How do we teach this creativity? I don't believe that Florida would say that such creativity can be taught; it must be cultivated. He reports that the university is the key institution for the creative economy, a "creative hub" that helps establish three qualities of a creative place: technology, talent, and tolerance (292). Universities are generally high-tech sites where innovations in technology research are constantly being developed; they attract talented researchers and graduate students; and they "help to create a progressive, open and tolerant people climate" (292). Such qualities help to sustain a creative economy in which individuals can produce innovations, improvements, and better ways of thinking.

How does writing connect with this "creative economy?" If our students are entering this economy and if this economy values the interconnection of all aspects of creativity, then our own distinctions and separations between types of writing and thinking (academic versus professional, for example) are out of sync with the creative ethos. We've already seen a push toward rethinking writing through creative means in the work of Geoffrey Sirc. Sirc's conception of composition as a happening falls in line with Florida's creative class and even with Taylor's network culture. Sirc's work seeks a (re)turn to avant-garde composition, and he takes the 1960s concept of the happening as the basis for this composition. "Happenings were all about blurring the boundaries of art and life," Sirc writes (9). In a sense, happenings are nodes that emerge within the cultural network of life through which we all connected. Nodes such as art, place, and time connect to produce something new and different. Sirc doesn't currently see much hope for creating something new and different within the current climate of Composition, partly due to the disciplinary borders that have been constructed: "Strict boundaries have become maintained in Composition, a separation of (profession-oriented) academy and life, one discipline from another, the specific discourse from a broader lived reality" (9). In contrast to this world of separation, he describes his book as "about the need to address deep, basic humanity in this modern over-sophisticated age" (31). Addressing that need involves validating forms of writing outside of traditional genres and forms that escape the academic and nonacademic monikers. Sirc offers his work in the hopes that Composition can shake off "more than a decade of conservative professionalism; to fracture our field's genres open for possibilities, risks, and material exploration, leading to a Composition in which hope and naiveté replace knowingness and expertise" (32). Sirc longs for the time before we were so invested in creating a discipline, when composition, as a general concept, could encompass a multitude of practices from art to writing to music. The current focus on academic discourse (and, I believe he would agree, the current push toward disciplinary status in professional writing) makes clear Composition's complicity with market values: "Composition, then, implicates itself in the contemporary re-figuring of education as training for work rather than intensification of experience" (8).

But must intensification and training be separate? As Florida seems to imply, creativity—certainly a type of intensity of experience—currently drives our economics. Could the ultimate training be the intensification of experience? One certainly hopes so. In many ways, what I am outlining might be enacted in the place or site we currently call an "independent writing program." But I'm not sure we need to adopt the rhetoric of independence to rethink the connections between creativity, intensity, and economics. Independence and stand-alone implies the attempt to forge a new ground away from the grounding of English, not to just escape the ground of English. It is not the same as Haynes's "writing offshore." And besides, do we really want to "stand-alone?" As Peggy O'Neill and Angela Crow note, there are problems with the concept of independence in the university. It may be necessary to develop momentum for change, but it is both "illusory" and a "fantasy" (4). O'Neill and Crow explain that "we always function in dependent ways in institutional systems" (4). The university, because it is an institution, is always going to limit what can and can't be done. Similarly, those restrictions can also function to merely replicate the same familiar structures within the new department or program. Yes, disciplinarity is invaluable for academic survival; however, the academy is itself changing, perhaps suggesting that it's not disciplinarity as an absolute that must diminish but our sense of how we shape, practice, and inhabit that disciplinarity. Thus, traditional disciplinarity runs counter to the current logic of the creative economy and of network culture. In short, it's *inhospitable*.

Threshold Spaces

Jacobs points us toward what he calls *threshold spaces*, places we can cultivate in order to foster a relationship of hospitality (572). We might also liken those spaces to sites without ground—in the middle, so to speak—and thus less available for disciplinary colonization. There are already some common threshold points, which can form hospitable connections between Composition Studies and professional writing. The first has been already discussed as one of the means by which the border between academic and nonacademic, expert and amateur, have collapsed: emerging technologies. Both Composition and professional writing share an interest in emerging media technologies, in particular Web 2.0 technologies that allow for simultaneous collaboration, commentary, production, and consumption. Such technologies are already affecting students' everyday lives, but they also affect professionals in the workplace. According to the Pew Research Center, about 72% of teens and young adults use social network sites compared with to 40% of adults (Lenhart et al). Moreover, social network sites are becoming an important place for professionals to network, share information about businesses, and promote products, often while serving entertainment and social purposes. In short, digital spaces, whether they are social networks, virtual worlds, forums, or just simple Web sites, cannot be easily characterized as professional or personal. The multitasking that we all do in online spaces indicates that digital media cannot be clearly divided into discrete functions or purposes. Indeed, this is true of our disciplines themselves as many of the scholars who define themselves as in areas such as computers and composition also work in professional writing.[11] The methods by which these scholars go about their research may be distinct, but not insurmountable, and in fact, I would argue that diverse research methodologies are critical for the development of new understandings. Thus, the digital work that professionals do is not so different from the work that first-year students do. An expansion of the idea of writing cannot ignore the kinds of "professional" writing that students are already doing.

Recent research by Bruce Horner and Min-Zhan Lu brings to light the ways that work can become a threshold uniting diverse areas of study. In "Working Rhetoric and Composition," they advocate "recognizing, and making more productive use of, relationships that *rhetoric and composition* might have with rhetorical study not affiliated with composition, and also with education and applied linguistics" (471). In their discussion, Horner and Lu include workplace writing and references to professional writing within what they call Rhetoric and Composition. While their essay's focus is on forging productive alliances with education and applied linguistics, it could also be extended to professional writing or even sites within communication. Horner and Lu acknowledge that the terms *rhetoric* and *composition* have diverse meanings and references, but that diversity can be considered a strength: "linking the three terms (*rhetoric*, *composition*, and *rhetoric and composition*) with a rich and changing array of practices, bodies of knowledge, and institutional sites can enhance the work of rhetoric and composition as an institutional space for developing alternatives and forms of resistance to hegemonic forces and relations" (473). Resisting hegemony is a commonality to be cultivated in both professional writing and Composition Studies, and here the distinction is not so much a lack of understanding as much as an issue of response. Composition asks how we can work against global capitalism; professional writing asks how we can acknowledge the constraints composed by global capitalism. A different way to form this question would be how we can work against the constraints composed by global capital, perhaps in different venues, such as within digital spaces or within communities.

A final threshold, and perhaps an overlooked one, is service learning. Both professional writing and Composition Studies share a commitment to bringing service learning, otherwise referred to as community engagement, to the classroom, and perhaps it is at this point where we might resolve issues with dealing with the capitalist impulse in higher education. But first, we need to engage in conversations about the scholarship in the field in productive ways. Thomas Deans, Barbara Roswell, and Adrian J. Wurr's recent collection of key sources on service learning, *Writing and Community Engagement: A Critical Sourcebook*, contains only one selection by a scholar in professional writing despite a large body of published research.[12] Because of this research, professional writing often cites its own sources rather than looking outside of itself toward Composition. But community engagement is a practice predicated on hospitality; it is the development of a relationship of trust and openness among teacher, student, institution, and community agency. Community engagement sites are almost always offshore locations, beyond the borders of the university, but they are also marginalized spaces within the community and the larger culture. Both professional writing and Composition scholars can engage such offshore locations not necessarily as disciplinary sites for application of expert knowledge but as community locations where they can enact and learn hospitality. As Jacobs reminds us, "Rhetorical listening and monastic hospitality require us to cultivate a radical sense of openness in our professional relationships, countering these established ways of operating and allowing us to move forward in productive ways" (577). While our two fields cannot and should not disappear or merge, they can become more hospitable as a way of moving forward productively and forging alliances when needed to achieve a common goal of fostering rhetorical sensibilities that push against traditional claim-driven problem-solving—a goal that dovetails with emerging technologies, creative and human commitments, and economic realities that describe network culture today.

Conclusion

"Language is hospitality," writes Derrida in a Levinasian move (135). Hospitality is the inviting and receiving of what seems strange or foreign to us. We locate some of this strangeness, as Johnson-Sheehan and Paine note, in the different languages of professional writing and Composition. But Derrida suggests that absolute, unconditional hospitality might "consist in suspending language, a particular determinate language, and even the address to the other. Shouldn't we also submit to a sort of holding back of the temptation to ask the other who he is, what her name is, where he comes from, etc.?" (135). This is the wonder and multiplicity of language. On the one hand, language allows us to welcome and invite, but on the other, suspending language can allow for the most hospitability. It is not a suspension of all language, but a forgetting of the language of *identification*, of disciplinarity—the language that declares us part of a group or allegiance. Giving up the language that defines us in terms of who we are not will open the doors for a yes to whatever comes. Our lack of hospitality between professional writing and Composition Studies is not insurmountable, but overcoming it does involve the willingness to stop trying to stake a claim, to occupy a ground that will change under their feet. This new hospitality must necessarily carry over into writing instruction. We might, with Haynes, ask if it is ethical for us to teach students to rely on argument "when *so much defies reason*" (669). A hospitable approach to writing (and, by extension, to one another) wants to go further. It does not require abandoning the safe harbors of reason, analysis, and critique, but it no longer feels bound by them either. No longer fearful of what lies in the offshore depths, it is, in fact, willing to plumb those depths in order to create something (a)new.

Before we can even think about teaching hospitable writing, we need to create the conditions of possibility for a potential solidarity between Composition and professional writing. This would mean leaving behind Composition's and professional writing's desires for status as all-knowing disciplines. It would mean an attention to "deep, basic humanity" (Sirc 31), an *abstract* concept that requires exploration in order for us to understand how to even think it. Part of what it means to think this concept would be to see that part of being human in a world of creativity and networks is adaptability. How do we teach adaptability in thinking, in writing? Our students already have adaptability as part of their existence. As Haynes points out, students are used to change, used to the constantly shifting ground: "forced mobility is constitutive of their constant movement from classroom to classroom, from pedagogy to pedagogy, from discipline to discipline, from technology to technology, from this settlement to that camp" (697). As professionals in Composition and professional writing, we are the ones who have a hard time adapting to change, to the stranger at the door. Let's open the gates of composition, of writing, with a newfound hospitality. After all, isn't adaptability all about being *hospitable* to change?

Notes

1 Victor Vitanza, Michelle Ballif, and Diane Davis, among others, have called Composition Studies to (re)turn to sophistry. In particular, Vitanza's "Seeing in Third Sophistic Ways" outlines this return to sophistry.

2 I use the term "professional writing" here to denote what might be more formally known as business and technical writing and communication. As a term, professional communication, according to Brenton Faber, "is used as a catchall term for various types of workplace and occupational writing" (306). Perhaps more provocatively, Jo Allen argues effectively for not defining technical writing, stating "no definition will adequately describe what we do" ("Case" 77).

3 Two essays come to mind as attempting to show the connections between professional writing and Composition Studies: David Russell's "Rethinking the Articulation between Business and Technical Communication and Writing in the Disciplines: Useful Avenues for Teaching and Research" and Jo Allen's "Bridge over Troubled Waters? Connecting Research and Pedagogy in Composition and Business/Technical Communication." While Russell's essay focuses more on writing in the disciplines, there are some overlaps with Composition Studies. Also, I might note that both of these pieces are in professional writing publications, and while there is some discussion in composition studies journals, there has been little direct connection between the two fields.

4 The same critique of argument in composition theory might also be leveled to genre in professional writing. Genre functions as the basis for much of what is taught in professional writing theory, but only recently are professional writing theorists acknowledging that genre is not as stable, as grounded, as we might like to believe.

5 See, for example, Dombrowski, "*Challenger* and the Social Contingency of

Meaning: Two Lessons for the Technical Communication Classroom."

6 We can clearly see the tension between ethics and persuasion in the infamous example discussed by Katz in "The Ethic of Expediency: Classical Rhetoric, Technology, and the Holocaust" and in recent critiques of Katz's article by Moore and Ward.

7 For a discussion of why we should be skeptical of attempts to map argument across hypertext structures, see my *JAC* response essay, "The Limits of Argument."

8 See her keynote address from CCCC, published as "Made Not Only in Words: Composition in a New Key."

9 During the 2010 MLA, Brian Croxall, a literature scholar, gained prominence by not giving his talk (due to financial difficulties) and having it spread via social networking.

10 Indeed, even in business and industry, professionals often "spoof" their own work. This is often seen in marketing departments of high-tech companies, which might spoof industry jargon or techspeak. The purpose here is for pure enjoyment, not to solve a problem or achieve a purpose.

11 The following scholars come to mind as being affiliated both with computers and composition and with professional writing: Michael Salvo, Jeff Grabill, Cynthia Selfe, Stuart Selber, and Dànielle DeVoss.

12 A quick keyword search for "service learning" in the journal *Technical Communication Quarterly* yields twelve results.

Works Cited

Allen, Jo. "Bridge over Troubled Waters? Connecting Research and Pedagogy in Composition and Business/Technical Communication." *Technical Communication Quarterly* 1.4 (1992): 5-26. Print.

———. "The Case Against Defining Technical Writing." *Journal of Business and Technical Communication* 4.2 (1990): 68-77. Print.

Aronowitz, Stanley. *The Knowledge Factory*. Boston: Beacon, 2000. Print.

Bay, Jennifer. "The Limits of Argument: A Response to Sean Williams." *JAC* 22.3 (2002): 684-697. Print.

Blakeslee, Ann M., and Rachel Spilka. "The State of Research in Technical Communication." *Technical Communication Quarterly* 13.1 (2004): 73-92. Print.

Deans, Thomas, Barbara Roswell, and Adrian J. Wurr. *Writing and Community Engagement: A Critical Sourcebook*. New York: Bedford/St. Martin's, 2010. Print.

Derrida, Jacques, and Anne Dufourmantelle. *Of Hospitality: Anne Dufourmantelle Invites Jacques Derrida to Respond*. Trans. Rachel Bowlby. Stanford: Stanford UP, 2000. Print.

Dombrowski, Paul. "*Challenger* and the Social Contingency of Meaning: Two Lessons for the Technical Communication Classroom." *Technical Communication Quarterly* 1.3 (1992): 73-86. Print.

Faber, Brenton. "Professional Identities: What is Professional about Professional Communication?" *Journal of Business and Technical Communication* 16.3 (2002): 306-337. Print.

Florida, Richard. *The Rise of the Creative Class*. New York: Basic Books, 2002. Print.

Frank, Thomas. *New Consensus for Old: Cultural Studies from Left to Right*. Chicago: Prickly Paradigm, 2002. Print.

Gillmor, Dan. *We the Media: Grassroots Journalism by the People, for the People*. Sebastapol: O'Reilly, 2004. Web. 22 Sept. 2010.

Grabill, Jeff. *Writing Community Change: Designing Technologies for Citizen Action*. Cresskill: Hampton, 2007. Print.

Haswell, Janis, Richard Haswell, and Glenn Blalock. "Hospitality in College Composition Courses." *CCC* 60.4 (2009): 707-727. Print.

Haynes, Cynthia. "Writing Offshore: The Disappearing Coastline of Composition Theory." *JAC* 23.4 (2003): 667-724. Print.

Horner, Bruce, and Min-Zhan Lu. "Working Rhetoric and Composition." *College English* 72.5 (2010): 470-494. Print.

Jacobs, Dale. "The Audacity of Hope." *JAC* 28.3-4 (2008): 563-581. Print.

Johnson-Sheehan, Richard, and Charles Paine. "Changing the Center of Gravity: Collaborative Writing Program Administration in Large Universities." *Technical Communication Quarterly* 13.2 (2004): 199-210. Print.

Katz, Steven. "The Ethic of Expediency: Classical Rhetoric, Technology, and the Holocaust." *College English* 54.3 (1992): 255-275. Print.

Lenhart, Amanda, Kristen Purcell, Aaron Smith, and Kathryn Zickuhr. "Social Media and Young Adults." *Pew Research Center's Internet and American Life Project*. 3 Feb. 2010. Web. 27 May 2010.

Mahala, Daniel, and Jody Swilky. "Constructing Disciplinary Space: The Borders, Boundaries, and Zones of English." *JAC* 23.4 (2003): 765-97. Print.

Moore, Patrick. "Questioning the Motives of Technical Communication and Rhetoric: Steven Katz's 'Ethic of Expediency.'" *Journal of Technical Writing and Communication* 34.1-2 (2004): 5-29. Print.

O'Neill, Peggy, and Angela Crow. "*Introduction*: Cautionary Tales About Change." Introduction. *A Field of Dreams: Independent Writing Programs and the Future of Composition Studies*. Ed. Peggy O'Neill, Angela Crow, and Larry W. Burton. Logan: Utah State UP, 2002. 1-20. Print.

Readings, Bill. *The University in Ruins*. Cambridge: Harvard UP, 1996. Print.

Royer, Daniel J., and Roger Gilles. "The Origins of a Department of Academic, Creative, and Professional Writing." *A Field of Dreams: Independent Writing Programs and the Future of Composition Studies*. Ed. Peggy O'Neill, Angela Crow, and Larry W. Burton. Logan: Utah State UP, 2002. 21-37. Print.

Russell, David. "Rethinking the Articulation between Business and Technical Communication and Writing in the Disciplines: Useful Avenues for Teaching and Research." *Journal of Business and Technical Communication* 21.3 (2007): 248-77. Print.

Salvo, Michael. "Ethics of Engagement: User-centered Design and Rhetorical Methodology." *Technical Communication Quarterly* 10.3 (2001): 273-290. Print.

Selber, Stuart. *Multiliteracies for a Digital Age*. Carbondale: Southern Illinois UP, 2004. Print.

Selfe, Cynthia. *Technology and Literacy in the Twenty-First Century: The Importance of Paying Attention*. Carbondale: Southern Illinois UP, 1999. Print.

Sirc, Geoffrey. *English Composition as a Happening*. Logan: Utah State UP, 2002. Print.

Taylor, Mark C. *The Moment of Complexity: Emerging Network Culture*. Chicago: U of Chicago P, 2002. Print.

Vitanza, Victor. "Seeing in Third Sophistic Ways." *Rhetoric and Composition as Intellectual Work*. Ed. Gary A. Olson. Carbondale: Southern Illinois UP, 2002. 164-74. Print.

Yancey, Kathleen Blake. "Made Not Only in Words: Composition in a New Key." *CCC* 56.2 (2004): 297-328. Print.

Ward, Mark. "The Banality of Rhetoric? Assessing Steven Katz's 'The Ethic of Expediency' Against Current Scholarship on the Holocaust." *Journal of Technical Writing and Communication* 39.2 (2009): 207-222. Print.

Changing Research Methods, Changing History: A Reflection on Language, Location, and Archive

Jessica Enoch

This essay reflects on the research methods the author employed to write three Chicana teachers into the history of rhetorical education. Her reflections ultimately push beyond her experience to explore how scholars can continue to research and investigate the pedagogies composed by and for marginalized populations at non-elite institutions. In taking up this work, however, she also exposes a number of unarticulated assumptions at the heart of historiographic practice that subtly shape research activities and prevent the diversification and expansion of research, writing, and thinking.

[W]hen we resist primacy, traditional paradigms for seeing and valuing participation, even in composition studies, are inadequate. They obviously miss the experiences and achievements of many, and they privilege by this process the viewpoints and the interpretations of the officialized few, whether they are acknowledged as prime or not. The challenge then is to broaden the research base, the inquiry base, the knowledge base from which interpretive frameworks can be drawn, not simply to say that we know we don't know but to do the work of finding out. We need methodologies for seeing the gaps in our knowledge and for generating the research that can help us fill those gaps.

    —Jacqueline Jones Royster and Jean C. Williams, "History in the Spaces Left," 1999 (582-3)

We do not at all mean that our children should not be taught the [English] language of the land that they live in, since it is the means that will enable them to communicate directly with their neighbors, and that will equip them to appreciate their rights. What we simply meant to say was that we ought not disregard the [Spanish] language, because it is the official stamp of the race and of the people.

    —Jovita Idar, "The Mexican Children in Texas," 1911 (1)

Over ten years ago, Jacqueline Jones Royster and Jean C. Williams called scholars in the field to take up two interrelated tasks. The first was to counter officialized disciplinary narratives by composing histories of Rhetoric and Composition that account for marginalized rather than enfranchised students and teachers, as well as nontraditional rather than elite writing programs and pedagogies. The second was to articulate the research methods and methodologies that enable this kind of critical work to come into being. Given the number of histories published over the last decade, the first call has been (and continues to be) answered, with scholars such as Anne Ruggles Gere, David Gold (*Rhetoric*), Susan Jarratt, Susan Kates, Shirley Wilson Logan (*Liberating*), Kelly Ritter, Lucille Schultz, and Stephen Schneider composing studies that enrich, expand, and complicate understandings of writing instruction in the United States.[1] In terms of Royster and Williams's second call, however, there has not been as vociferous a response. While scholars have surely discussed larger issues of historiographic method and methodology, we have not spent as much time articulating and analyzing the *particular* research strategies that allow us to tell a "reconfigured, more fully textured story" of our field's past (Royster and Williams 581).[2]

This essay takes up this latter challenge by identifying and reflecting on the research methods I used to write three teachers, Jovita Idar, Marta Peña, and Leonor Villegas de Magnón, into the history of rhetorical education. In the fourth chapter of *Refiguring Rhetorical Education: Women Teaching African American, Native American, and Chicano/a Students, 1865-1911*, I analyze the pedagogical arguments these women made through the pages of *La Crónica*, a turn-of-the-century, Spanish-language newspaper serving Laredo, Texas, that was owned and operated by Idar and her family. As the epigraph above indicates, Idar and her colleagues used the press to call for educational practices that embraced the Spanish language, asserted cultural knowledge, and reformulated civic duties. Their educational articles taught readers to envision themselves as active agents who could promote Mexican cultural traditions while negotiating the realities of their increasingly Anglo and discriminatory Texas society. In assessing their work, I argue that Idar, Peña, and Villegas offered their readers a resistant rhetorical education by providing them with the discursive skills as well as the civic and cultural knowledge necessary not just to participate in, but also to re-shape their Laredo, Texas community. Thus, I use the chapter in my book to claim that because these women composed such revolutionary pedagogical practices inside the pages of *La Crónica*, their work should revise our understandings of how rhetorical education has occurred in this country.

In this article, I shift my scholarly emphasis to meditate on the research methods that enabled me to write about these teachers and trouble dominant narratives of rhetorical education. It is important to note that my focus in this essay is on methods rather than methodology. Gesa Kirsch and Patricia Sullivan identify the distinction between these terms, writing that while methodology concerns itself with the "underlying theory and analysis of how research does or should proceed," methods are the "techniques or ways of proceeding in gathering evidence" (2). Of course, it is almost impossible to separate completely these two concepts—our theory surely informs the ways we choose to gather evidence and vice versa. But in focusing attention on method, we gain insight on the specific practices that enable us to produce a research project: the work of "locat[ing] and using primary materials [. . . and] achieving access to information" (ĽEpplattenier, "Opinion" 69). As Barbara ĽEpplattenier explains, "methods make the invisible work of historical research visible" (69). By making research methods visible, we attain a clearer sense of what historians are and are not doing when they compose their narratives. And, through this atomistic view, we have the opportunity to assess the practices that open up and close down historiographic possibilities, learning more about the methodological thruways and roadblocks that allow for and prevent alternative histories to be composed.

This meditation on my research methods ultimately aims to "broaden the research base, the inquiry base, the knowledge base from which interpretive frameworks can be drawn," so that scholars in the field can continue to compose histories that center on marginalized populations and non-elite institutions (Royster and Williams 581). To do this work, I use the major sections of the essay to reflect on the three research methods that I believe distinguished my work: choosing a Spanish-language newspaper as a primary text; locating a history of rhetorical education at the border city of Laredo, Texas; and conducting research at the Webb County Historical Foundation, a small community archive in Laredo. As I make these reflections, I consider how each method brings to light a number of unarticulated assumptions that lie at the heart of traditional historiographic methods. These assumptions not only stand at the center of much historiographic work, but also have the potential to stand in the way of historiographic exploration and revision. My work here, then, is to interrogate these assumptions, suggesting new ways to gather and assess historiographic evidence.

Primary Texts *en Español*

The road that led me to choose *La Crónica* as a primary text was a bumpy and circuitous one. As a doctoral student at Penn State University, I embarked on a dissertation project that examined the work of female teachers at the turn of the twentieth century. By 1912, the teaching profession had become an "Adamless Eden," and I was interested in learning more about the pedagogical practices of all of these "Eves" (Bardeen 18). More specifically, I wanted to interrogate the historiographic "fact" that the female teacher was an innocuous nurturer disinterested in the politics of education. So I began my research by looking to moments of conflict when teachers had to address questions of gender, race, culture, and power. The Mexican Revolution was one such moment. This period, I believed, could enable me to explore how teachers living on the Texas-Mexico border responded not just to the influx of Mexican immigrants to Texas, but also to the questions of nation, citizenship, culture, politics, and language that arrived with them.[3]

Thus, I began my research by reading secondary materials about Mexican education in Texas, searching for references and footnotes that would lead to the field-specific artifacts valued by scholars in Rhetoric and Composition Studies such as textbooks, pedagogical materials, and collections of student papers. Time and again I came up with nothing. Disheartened, I felt as if my work was only reifying the "myth of Mexican indifference" that Guadalupe San Miguel Jr. writes about: the idea that "Mexican Americans have not really cared for education or else they have failed to appreciate its importance and benefit to their community in particular and to the society at large" (xvi). Wanting to challenge this myth, I turned to other secondary materials, this time looking for texts that addressed more general themes of Mexican political activity. Finally, I got my lead when I came across Jose Limón's 1974 essay "*El Primer Congreso Mexicanista de 1911*: A Precursor to Chicanismo." In this article, Limón refers to the Spanish-language newspaper *La Crónica* as a "remarkable newspaper" that not only was dedicated to the "industrial, moral, and intellectual development" of Mexican people living in Texas, but also was concerned with the particular problem of educational discrimination in the state's public schools (87, 88). Limón referenced the fact that the Idar family owned the press, with daughter Jovita Idar serving as an editor and contributor.

Eager to learn more about the educational agenda of the newspaper and Idar's involvement in it, I requested the microfilm of the newspaper through interlibrary loan. Once I received the microfilm, a quick skim of its contents assured me that this was no dead end. On page after page, *La Crónica* printed articles in which writers spoke out against school discrimination and offered arguments for change. It railed against Americanization programs that enforced the English language and Anglo culture. It publicized Laredo's *escuelitas,* the small, community-run schools often headed by female teachers that offered bilingual and bicultural education. And it functioned as an educational space itself, using its pages to teach readers about language, cultural, and civic issues. It did not take long for me to realize that I should pursue this text further, so I embarked on the rewarding and labor-intensive task of translating over 60 articles from the newspaper and focusing attention on the three teachers, Idar, Peña, and Villegas, whose pedagogical arguments spoke significantly to pressing questions about language, literacy, culture, and civic participation that circulate in the field today.[4]

The rewards in choosing *La Crónica* as a primary text prompt us to consider an obvious yet unarticulated research method central to our field's historiographic work. Scholars who compose histories that investigate writing and rhetorical instruction in the U.S. certainly consult a wide range of primary materials. While more traditional or "curricular" histories rely on lecture notes, course descriptions, department meeting minutes, and so on, "extracurricular" histories—histories of those spaces *outside* the university where writing and rhetorical instruction occurs—place under examination a different, more varied collection of materials, such as conduct books, club papers, newspapers, and parlor rhetorics (see Gere, "Kitchen"). In consulting an ever-widening range of materials, historians continually redefine what "counts" as a resource that could provide insight to past practice. It is important to note, however, that with few exceptions these texts have one thing in common: they are all written in English.[5] Because of this singular focus on primary texts written in English, our investigations into the history of rhetoric and writing instruction have so far only told one part of a much larger story.

Bruce Horner and John Trimbur write that the field of Composition has consistently enforced a "unidirectional monolingual language policy" through the teaching of writing in English only (607). My work with *La Crónica* reveals that this univocal monolingual language policy also directs our research practices. Stories like those of the teachers in my study are often not told because we focus our research efforts on texts written in English. Further investigations of Spanish-language newspapers alone would most likely confirm my contention that the implicit and expected monolingualism of our field's research methods necessarily limit our understandings of the history of language and rhetorical instruction. For, even though the pedagogical work of Idar, Peña, and Villegas was exemplary, it was not extraordinary. There are certainly more texts like *La Crónica* to be studied.

As Herminio Rios and Guadelupe Castillo have found, prior to 1940 there were 372 Spanish-language newspapers published in the southwest region that includes Arizona, Texas, Colorado, New Mexico, and California (Cortés 248).[6] This number does not take into account those presses created in Spanish-speaking enclaves in cities such as Chicago, New York, Tampa, and Miami, or those newspapers published after 1940 and especially during the 1960s that Spanish-speaking students composed at both the high school and college levels (253). Scholars such as Carlos Cortés, Félix Gutiérrez, Doris Meyer, and América Rodriguez have pinpointed the various functions of these publications. While some were more accomodationist and simply translated Anglo news for Spanish-speaking readers, others, like *La Crónica,* espoused a more bicultural and activist stance, speaking out as defenders of the community and as agitators against Anglo discrimination. This latter group often worked as "preservers of Chicano history and culture, maintainers and enforcers of language, and strengtheners of Chicano pride" (Cortés 255). As Meyer explains, by taking on the "unofficial role of public forum and community bulletin board," revolutionary newspapers often became sites "where aggrieved citizens could speak out" (406). In terms of the use and regard for the Spanish (and English) language, Cortés outlines the differing positions these presses adopted—positions that reflect their political and cultural investments:

Some use only traditional Spanish; others champion the use of variations of Chicano Spanish or even bilingual writing that integrates Spanish and English words, sometimes within the same sentence and particularly in poetry. English-language Chicano publications have sometimes functioned as instruments of social activism, cultural reflection, and historical preservation, yet they obviously have contributed little to Spanish language usage in the United States. (255)

As a field, then, we might turn our attention to newspapers such as *El Mexicano, La República, La Voz de América, El Mercurio de Nueva York, La Prensa, La Opinión, Las Novedades, Vida Obrera, La Luz, El Obrero, La Mujer Moderna, La Voz de la Mujer,* and *El Progreso*.[7] And these selections are just the beginning since I've only catalogued here Spanish-language presses. Presses published in other languages and by other cultural communities would likely yield similar results. Even so, by investigating just these Spanish-language publications and choosing them as primary texts for historiographic investigation, we would not only enrich our understanding of how Spanish-speaking communities addressed educational debates, but we would also be able to place college writing and rhetoric instruction in a broader context.

In recent years, scholars such as Horner, Trimbur, Paul Matsuda, and Amy Zenger have worked to establish how and why English-language instruction gained prominence in the U.S. university system. For example, Horner and Trimbur investigate the "protracted struggle" (597) that eventually positioned English as the *lingua franca* of the university through a drastic reduction in attention to classical languages and the "territorializ[ation]" of modern languages like French, German, and Spanish to "separate departments where students encountered [these languages] as texts to be read, not living languages to be written or spoken" (602). Matsuda extends this conversation, arguing that since its inception, the first-year composition course has functioned as a site of "linguistic containment, quarantining from the rest of higher education students who have not yet been socialized into the dominant linguistic practices" (641). And Zenger's study of student themes at Harvard explains how "required writing, reading, and critiquing" in English was a "means of negotiating a racially inflected identity: speaker of English as the mother tongue" (333).

These studies are revealing in that they chronicle how the composition classroom and the university became sites primarily invested in English-language instruction. However, placed in a broader context and in conversation with educational debates waged in non-English-language publications like *La Crónica,* this university initiative gains a different nuance: we can understand it as one voice in a multi-vocal and multilingual conversation about language instruction in the United States. Right at the moment when English became the dominant language of the university, *La Crónica* contributors were speaking out against Americanization campaigns that pinpointed English instruction as a vital part of their programs. Indeed, this broader view allows us to see that instruction in English at the college level did not "merely emerg[e] by default to fill the vacuum left by the classical languages" (Zenger 338). Instead, this shift in university priorities worked in concert with a nationwide Americanization movement that greatly affected educational initiatives at all levels both inside and outside the university.

Thus, choosing non-English language documents as primary texts for historiographic exploration has the potential to reap significant rewards. In terms of research methods, though, the choice requires that we do the difficult work of adding a new "too[l] to the historians' trade" (Ferreira-Buckley 582). As a field, we need to gain greater proficiency in languages other than English. It would only make sense that if we want to learn more about those who spoke to their communities about alternative, non-English language pedagogies or those who advocated for bicultural and bilingual education, we would need to consult texts written in the languages of those writers and their communities.

Of course, for many, studying non-English language texts is not easy; therefore, institutional support would help scholars to add this tool to their trade. For instance, individual departments or national institutions such as NCTE or CCCC might consider offering grants that would assist researchers in translating materials. Graduate courses might focus attention on the "ethnic press" as part of Rhetoric and Composition's extracurricular history. Graduate programs might encourage study in translation courses, comparative literature departments, and other modern language departments. And they might also take language requirements more seriously. As Doug Steward writes, the language requirement has become little more than a hoop to jump through because few English departments stress research in foreign languages (209-10). Rhetoric and Composition programs in particular might re-see this requirement as an opportunity for graduate students to translate educational texts and extracurricular materials that could give insight to alternative pedagogical practices or educational debates. By creating these opportunities for researchers, and especially for graduate students, our field would put scholars in the position to broaden the selection of primary texts we are able to consult and, accordingly, deepen and diversify the histories we produce.

Historiographic Locations

As scholars such as Gesa Kirsch and Christine Sutherland have made clear, going "on location" and actually visiting the places and spaces where historical subjects lived and wrote is an "invaluable" scholarly experience and research method (Kirsch, "Being" 20). For although we can never go back to the moment of inquiry and see what our subjects saw, the process of inhabiting their same spaces and places allows us to get "into closer touch" with their worlds, enabling us to piece the historiographic puzzle together more effectively and efficiently (Sutherland 29).

Kirsch and Sutherland's assessments of this research practice certainly resonates with my own. While reading *La Crónica* articles in Penn State's microfilm room—almost 1,800 miles from Laredo—I continually encountered references to Nuevo Laredo, Laredo's sister city on the Mexican side of the border; contributors frequently mentioned the Rio Grande, and they consistently wrote of their travels from Texas to Mexico and back again. Looking at Laredo's location on the map, I could see that since the city was a border town, it would make sense that Mexico and cities on the other side of the border would figure into *La Crónica* writers' contributions. These references, however, gained new meaning once I traveled to Laredo and saw the city and its location with my own eyes.

The moment I arrived in Laredo, I realized that Mexico, Nuevo Laredo, and the Rio Grande were not just sites that were close by or in the same general vicinity. Mexico is a physical presence that is visible from Laredo's city center: the border, the river, and Nuevo Laredo are all within eyesight of Laredo's streets. Being there and assessing Laredo's proximity to Mexico enabled me to understand not only what contributors were referring to but also why these references were so persistent: one could not live in Laredo without acknowledging the presence of Mexico and its border. Simple as it might seem, this observation crystallized understandings about geographic locations that have the potential to expand and challenge our historiographic work.

When researching writing programs and pedagogies from the past, historians often take into account a number of variables that might have affected the way instruction was conducted. We consider the classed, raced, cultured, and gendered status of teachers and students; we assess their use of and access to textbooks and other pedagogical materials; and we reflect on the educational, social, and political climate of the moment. We often do not, however, consider how geographic location inflects pedagogical practice.

Walking the streets of Laredo helped me realize how important a role location can play in pedagogical production; living on the border of Texas and Mexico shaped every aspect of Idar's, Peña's, and Villegas's work. Just as they and their readers crossed and re-crossed the Rio Grande, their pedagogies borrowed and built from both Mexican and American worlds. Ultimately, though, these women's teaching practices were not an even mixture of national and cultural imperatives; instead they were distinctive of and individual to the particular border space in which they lived. For instance, while they argued for their rights as U.S. citizens, they taught readers about Mexican citizenship and culture. And as they rejected English-Only instruction, they did not advocate for Spanish-only instruction but called instead for bilingual and bicultural education in Texas schools. It was because Idar, Peña, and Villegas wrote and taught in what Gloria Anzaldúa defines as the "b"orderlands—the "actual physical borderland" or geographic space where cultures meet—that they created complex pedagogical practices distinguished by powerful and unique cultural and civic negotiations (19). [8]

Nedra Reynolds and Vorris Nunley have convincingly argued that "rhetorical scholarship has undertheorized how spatiality, the politics and poetics of space, mediate rhetorical performances" (Nunley 222). Given my work in Laredo and with Idar, Peña, and Villegas, I extend this claim, adding that historical scholarship in the field has undertheorized how spatiality and geography have affected pedagogical practice. Heidemarie Weidner's research counts as one exception. In her investigation of nineteenth-century composition instruction at Butler University in Indianapolis, Indiana, she writes that because Butler was "situated at what was then the western frontier [. . .] it differed greatly from the eastern schools" (60):

> Less inflexible, more convinced of the necessity to adapt to rapid changes brought on by a growing western expansion [, . . . educators] found it easier to choose curricular change, a decision which resulted in a dynamic, community-centered and practical education. (60)

Here, we see that by attending to questions of location, Weidner can offer a fuller explanation of *why* Butler's program developed as it did. Thus, the research practice of going "on location" does more than allow us to do the important work of making sense of oblique references or experiencing, in some small way, the worlds of our historical subjects. It also gives us the opportunity to ask larger questions about how the geographic location of the educational site affected the pedagogy produced there.

This awareness of the ways place interanimates pedagogy prompts consideration of another research method: that of choosing a historiographic location. Certainly, Royster and Williams along with Gere have articulated the value of relocating historical studies outside the campuses of prestigious universities, and scholars have in great numbers proven this point true by examining pedagogies produced in Historically Black Colleges, labor colleges, women's colleges, and normal schools as well as parlors, kitchen tables, and rented rooms. Locating my research on the borderlands of Texas and Mexico, however, made me realize that our frame of reference regarding location needs to get incrementally larger because our histories of rhetoric and writing instruction are often situated within a specific and unarticulated terrain. We not only often situate histories at university sites, but we often locate them in the Northeast corner of the United States.

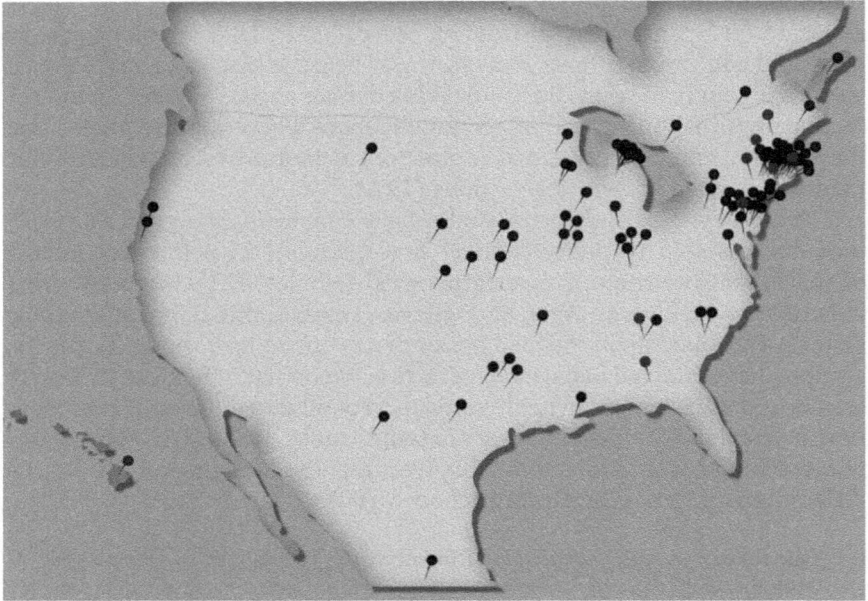

Figure 1: *This map plots the historiographic locations examined in 70 studies of rhetoric and writing instruction.*

Figure 1 confirms this point, demonstrating that our disciplinary field is not an abstract one. Out of 70 histories surveyed, scholars have conducted research at 126 curricular and extracurricular sites. Of this total number, 71 historiographic locations are situated along the Northeastern seaboard of the U.S., with an additional 11 studies based at the University of Michigan. Forty-five studies are located outside the "hotbed" of Rhetoric and Composition, with only three engaging work in the Southwest region of North America (see Appendix for the studies I consulted to compose the map).

In creating this map I am not arguing that important and groundbreaking research on marginalized students and teachers cannot happen when scholars situate study in the Northeast, but I am asserting that our field's historiographic understandings have the potential to be enriched if we looked beyond this region. For, if place does indeed inform pedagogy, our histories of writing instruction are eclipsed when we, by and large, only locate our work in one geographic area. Moreover, since as a field we have committed ourselves to exploring contact zones, *metaphorical* "B"orderlands, transnational as well as multicultural agendas, we might consider how situating our study at *actual* borderlands like those of Laredo might invigorate our contemporary pedagogical questions, enabling us to learn more about how historical figures living in these spaces taught and learned about rhetoric and writing as well as cultural and civic engagement. By situating our research at new locations, then, we would adopt research methods that challenge disciplinary boundaries and reinforce our theoretical agendas.

As we take up this work, however, we should be critical of our methodological stance and especially of the metaphors we use to conceptualize our research. Reynolds explains that "spatial metaphors" carry with them "certain consequences" (27) in that they often "reflect and construct accepted ways of knowing" (5). Therefore, we should not see this attention to geographic location as an invitation to adopt a colonialist mentality and define our practice as one of *exploring new frontiers* or examining *untouched* places. Instead, our prerogative would be to question the boundaries and borders of our disciplinary field, approaching historiographic study with these questions in mind: Where do we implicitly argue that rhetoric and composition happens? What spaces does our field deem worth studying? How might other places and spaces complicate our understanding of writing and rhetorical instruction? By asking and answering these questions, we would come closer to realizing James Murphy's contention that "the place where one stands will have a great influence on what the historian's lever can move" (5). Location matters. Not only does our choice of location condition who and what we're able to see and study, but location itself also inflects the aims and interests of teachers and students, having the potential to act as a major factor in the overarching pedagogical project.

The Community Archive

Most historiographic research is not complete without a visit to an archive. Thus, I complemented my translations of *La Crónica* and my trip to Laredo with a visit to the Webb County Heritage Foundation (WCHF) to conduct the archival research that would deepen my understanding of Idar, Peña, and Villegas's work. I was especially hopeful that research at this archive would be successful because, in terms of my secondary and primary research, I had found little information about the women in my study besides a small number of scholarly articles on the Idar family and Villegas as well as the republication of Villegas's autobiography, *The Rebel*. Additionally, these women's names were all but absent from records at major research institutions such as the Library of Congress or the archives at the University of Texas. My hope, then, was that the WCHF, a local, community archive, would contain rich turn-of-the-twentieth-century materials about these women, their teachings, *La Crónica,* and life in Laredo that would allow me to recover these teachers' forgotten voices and bring their words to "full volume" (Logan, "Introduction" xi). What I found shifted my thinking about the conventional ways scholars of rhetoric and composition discuss their approaches to and work in the archive.

In my research at the WCHF, I certainly found compelling materials that made it possible for me to advance an argument about the revolutionary teaching practices of Idar, Peña, and Villegas. Just as interesting as these findings, however, was my realization that although these women were missing from our scholarly conversations, they were not forgotten inside the city of Laredo. When I entered the WCHF and inquired about Idar, Peña, and Villegas, the archivist did not immediately bring out turn-of-the-twentieth century documents. Rather, she presented me with *recent* newspaper clippings, public service announcements, and exhibit promotions that the Foundation itself had produced about Idar and Villegas.[9]

For instance, in 1992, the WCHF published a series of biographical sketches entitled "Celebration of our Heritage: Important Women in Webb County's History" for the city's local newspaper, the *Laredo Morning Times,* and both Idar and Villegas were featured in the series. In Idar's segment, community members learned that she was both a local teacher who "did not have enough text books, or benches or chairs, and on cold days no heat" ("Jovita" 8D) and a community activist who participated in the first Mexican Congress, *El Primer Congreso Mexicanista*; began a feminist organization, *La Liga Feminista Mexicanista*;[10] and formed, with Villegas, *Cruz Blanca* ("The White Cross"), which offered nursing aid to soldiers fighting in the Mexican Revolution. Similarly, in Villegas's installment, the Foundation defined her as a teacher and a political revolutionary—a woman who wrote "fiery speeches" in support of Mexican leader Francisco Madero ("Leonor" 5D).

The WCHF did not just use this series to educate the community about the historical significance of Idar and Villegas. As it informed readers about important women in Laredo's past, it also linked these figures to influential women in Laredo's present-day community.

> The women of Webb County have many times been forgotten in their contribution to the betterment of life in Webb County. Many [w]omen today contribute to the educational wealth and richness of Webb County. This article is dedicated to the 3 women who helped provide the material for this article who are contributing daily to the betterment of hundreds of Laredoans. They are Rose Trevino, Texas Archeological Steward; Dr. Norma Cantu, Laredo State University; and Prof. Lucy Cardenas, Laredo Junior College. ("Jovita" 8D)

In addition to this 1992 series on important Webb County women both past and present, the WCHF also celebrated the work of Villegas six years later by creating a photo exhibit of her kindergarten students and inviting Clara Lomas, Chicana scholar and editor of Villegas's autobiography, to speak at the event. The Foundation once again used this opportunity to connect community members to the history it presented. As one article in the *Laredo Weekly Times* explains, "Many Laredoans are sure to find themselves, a dear friend, or relative among these memorable photographs" ("Heritage Foundation Slates" 6D).

This effort to encourage community members to connect to and take part in their local history is even more pronounced in other Foundation events and programs. For instance, the WCHF works with local schools and universities to support an oral history project in which students interview community members and then contribute the interviews to the archive. It sponsored a "Save Our Story" campaign which "encourage[d] Laredo, Webb County, and border residents to bring forward their old photographs, documents, letters, maps, and artifacts to be assessed by staff with the possible option of loan or gift to the Webb County Heritage Foundation" ("Heritage," *Register* 8). And, it also awards the "President of the Rio Grande Scholarship," a $500 scholarship to students who produce essays on their family history.

The innovative work of the WCHF, and other archives like it, calls us to think about how we conceive of both ourselves as researchers and our research methods when conducting work at local, community archives as opposed to large, research institutions. In initial histories of Composition, James Berlin, Robert Connors (*Composition*), Sharon Crowley, John Brereton, and Albert Kitzhaber consistently consulted resources in university libraries such as those at Harvard, Yale, Iowa, and Michigan. "Our" archives were special collections at these sites, which preserved "those rarest and most valuable of data, actual student writings, teacher records, unprinted notes and pedagogical materials, and ephemera that writing courses have generated but rarely kept" (Connors, "Dreams" 225). As Connors explains in "Dreams and Play: Historical Method and Methodology," the conventional archival practice at these sites is one in which the researcher enters the archive with a specific question in mind and pursues this question, in many ways, like a hunter or a detective.

Connors first equates the researcher with the hunter, writing that she goes to the archive because of a "human instinct to make sense of things [. . . . She] enter[s] that jungle because there is something to track" (226). As the detective, the researcher searches for "inert archival materials" (225) and "dusty mass[es] of past records" (227) to find clues that might offer evidence concerning the mysteries of the past. Once this hunter/detective tracks down her prey or discovers her clues, she activates these materials in ways that help scholars of rhetoric and composition understand who we are and why we teach the way we do. The purpose of working in the archive and writing our history, Connors explains, is for us to tell "stories about the tribe to make the tribe real. [. . .] [W]e are telling the stories of our fathers and mothers, and we are legitimating ourselves through legitimating them" (234).

Such archival practices might make sense for a researcher working in a university archive that holds materials directly related to rhetoric and composition instruction. However, as scholars investigate alternative sites for instruction that often occurred outside university classrooms, they have expanded the range of archives they visit, turning their attention to smaller, local archives like the WCHF as a means to locate materials that would enhance their research. Researching at these archives requires different kinds of approaches than those scholars have used in more traditional archival settings.

My experiences at the WCHF suggest that we might first, as with the historiographic locations, recast the metaphors we use to define our practice in the archive. Seeing the WCHF as an unexplored jungle in need of taming or a crime scene where the researcher-detective discovers clues to a mystery might condition us to ignore the important civic and communal work of archives like the WCHF. The WCHF certainly functions as a place for historic preservation, but it also serves a site for communal involvement and civic engagement. The WCHF is an archive alive with contributions that community members compose, and it is a place where public memory in Laredo is constantly created and re-created. Moreover, the WCHF is not simply a library where scholars can research and compose histories of rhetoric and writing instruction. The WCHF is itself an extracurricular educational space: one of its objectives is to teach the community about its history while also connecting its past to Laredo's present and future. Therefore, as researchers continue to visit local and community archives like the WCHF, it is important that we avoid seeing ourselves as detectives or hunters. We might instead recognize that we are often outsiders to these communities whose members have leveraged very different arguments from these archives and about the figures we study.

This understanding of the work that happens in archives like the WCHF should especially inform the ways we see and "reclaim" figures like Idar, Peña, and Villegas. Through our historiography, we might indeed pinpoint women like these as foremothers whose voices we want to bring to *full volume* as a means to enrich our knowledge of past iterations of rhetorical education. But we also need to be cognizant of the fact that as teachers of rhetoric and composition, we are not their direct descendents; these women are not figures like Gertrude Buck, Mina Shaughnessy, or Anne Berthoff. Rather, we must appreciate the fact that through the interpretive work of the WCHF, Idar and Villegas are mothers of different lineages; they have been identified as part of a long line of female leaders in the community that continues from 1911 into the present moment. We might be "telling stories of the rhetoric and composition tribe" when we write the work of Idar, Peña, and Villegas into our disciplinary histories, but we should also not forget what other stories women like these are part of and what other kinds of significance they hold.

Reflecting critically on both the metaphors we use to define archival work and the ways we conceive our historical subjects ultimately helps us acknowledge that archives like the WCHF are not "our" archives. These are not spaces like Harvard's holdings of student papers, the Richard Beal collection at the Universities of New Hampshire and Rhode Island, or the Rhetoric and Composition Sound Archives at Texas Christian University. Because they are not "our" archives, scholars need to consider how their role as researchers means they do more than write about their subjects in ethical, respectful, and accurate ways. Researching in spaces other than those we might deem as our own means that we have special responsibilities in terms of the work we do there.

One responsibility of working in the community archive is that we learn not just about the figures relevant to our study but also about the archive itself and the function it serves inside its community: How and why have community members created and shaped the archive? What are its priorities and objectives? What kinds of arguments do archivists and community members create from the historical materials held in the archive? How do figures important to rhetoric and composition "figure into" their community's history and public memory? In answering these questions it does not mean that we paralyze ourselves from conducting our research, but it does mean that we don't just take materials and run.

The challenge of working in the community archive is that we look up from our own research and see the *other* kinds of work being done in and through the archive. As my experiences at the WCHF make clear, this kind of archive often takes up important communal, civic, and activist work. It is our objective as researchers to learn about this work and to see how our scholarship could reinforce or contribute to these initiatives. Such archival practices underscore and extend the point Royster makes in *Traces of a Stream* when she writes that "whatever knowledge accrued" through our research should be "presented and represented within th[e] community," making it possible for communal "participation and response" (274). It is the responsibility of the researcher that she "speak and interpret *with* the community, not just *for* the community, or *about* the community" (275). By speaking *with* archivists about the communal and civic goals of their archive, we elaborate on what counts as a research method. In addition to accessing and retrieving information, we must also see as viable and important the acts of sharing our research and writing with archivists, listening to them, and learning more about what the information we retrieve says not just about our history but about their community's past, present, and future.

New Methods, New Histories

Recent discussions about research methods offer sage advice and important information to scholars interested in conducting historiographic study. From Katherine Tirabassi, Wendy Sharer, Sammie Morris, and Shirley Rose, we learn about the archivist's work and the "organizing principles that gover[n] the construction, maintenance, and investigation of an archival collection" (Tirabassi 171). From Chris Warnick, we learn how to negotiate the various finding aids that might lead to promising primary resources. From Lynée Gaillet, we learn about funding opportunities that enable scholars to go "on location." And from David Gold we learn how to "embrace" and make the best use of serendipitous moments in the archive (see "Accidental").

My work in this essay contributes to and extends this conversation by considering how our investment in articulating research methods might be combined with the field's dedicated interest in composing alternative histories of rhetoric and writing instruction. In combining these interests, I see that we have an opportunity to, in the words of Royster and Williams, "se[e] the gaps in our knowledge" and "generat[e] the research that can help us fill those gaps" (581). But rethinking the language of primary texts, the location where we situate our research, and the practices we use to conduct archival research at local archives is just a start. The goal here is to invite others to the conversation so that we can continue to create new opportunities for listening to new voices and learning about new pedagogies because by changing our methods we change our histories.

Acknowledgements

I greatly appreciate the challenging revision suggestions of the three anonymous reviewers who helped me to rethink my work in this essay.

Notes

1 See also Patricia Donahue and Gretchen Fletcher Moon's collection, *Local Histories: Reading the Archives of Composition*.

2 For broad-based discussions of historiography in Rhetoric and Composition, see Octalog I and II, Anne Ruggles Gere ("Kitchen"), and Victor Vitanza. For specific discussions of archival methods and methodologies, see Barbara L'Eplattenier ("Opinion" and "Questioning"); Cheryl Glenn and Jessica Enoch; Gesa Kirsch and Liz Rohan; Alexis Ramsey et al.; Wendy Sharer; Barbara Biesecker; Charles E. Morris II; and the 1999 special issue of *College English*, *Archivists with an Attitude*.

3 This is not to say that there were no Mexican people living in the borderlands before this time. The region has been populated by Mexican people for hundreds of years. It was only because of the Texas Revolution of 1836 and the annexation of Texas to the United States that Mexican citizens became Americans when the border "literally migrated" over them (Zavella 77). The Revolution

years are exigent for study because of the pressing questions and concerns having to do with political turmoil, war, poverty, immigration, and citizenship that teachers had to contend with.

4 My thanks goes to Penn State University and the University of New Hampshire for funding the work of three fantastic translators, Lisa Lawson, Malena Florin, and Raquel Moran Tellez, who aided me in reading and transcribing these materials.

5 My focus here is on histories of Rhetoric and Composition in the U.S. Surely, histories of rhetoric rely on texts composed in languages other than English. I would contend, however, that these histories focus primarily on texts written in Latin, Greek, and other European languages and rarely consult those written in languages emerging from North and South America. Susan Romano's article "Tlaltelolco: The Grammatical-Rhetorical *Indios* of Colonial Mexico" serves as one exception.

6 For a recent study of *Mexican* women journalists in Mexico, see also Cristina D. Ramírez, "Forging a Mestiza Rhetoric."

7 Félix Gutiérrez provides a number of bibliographic resources that point researchers to archives that hold Spanish-language publications. See "Spanish-Language Newspaper Holdings" in the Barker Texas History Collection, University of Texas at Austin; Michael Randall, "Chicano Studies Serials Holdings at UCLA," Univeristy of California at Los Angeles Library; and Ricardo Chabrán, "Listing of 143 Chicano Publications on Microfilm," Chicano Studies Library, University of California at Berkeley (67). In addition, Ramón Gutiérrez's "The UCLA Bibliographic Survey of Mexican-American Literary Culture, 1821-1945: An Overview" would also be helpful in conducting this kind of research.

8 In *Feminist Rhetorical Theories,* Karen A. Foss, Sonja K. Foss, and Cindy L. Griffin explain the difference between Anzaldua's borderlands and Borderlands: "Written lowercase, the word refers to a geographic site—the 'actual southwest borderlands or any borderlands between two cultures.' When she capitalizes it, however, she is using it as a 'metaphor, not actuality' to refer to a state that exists whenever cultural differences exist, whether those cultures involve physical differences such as race, class, or gender, or differences that are less tangible—psychological, social, or cultural" (106).

9 Unfortunately, I was unable to find any secondary materials on Marta Peña. The only information I have about her life and work was culled through the contributions she made to *La Crónica* and references to her work as a teacher in the same newspaper.

10 To learn more about Idar's feminist investments as well as those of other Laredo women, see Jessica Enoch, "*Para la Mujer:* Defining a Chicana Feminist Rhetoric at the Turn of the Century."

Works Cited

Anzaldúa, Gloria. *Borderlands/La Frontera: The New Mestiza.* 2nd ed. San Francisco: Aute Lute, 1999. Print.

Archivists with an Attitude. Spec. issue of *College English* 61.5 (1999): 574-98. Print.

Bardeen, C.W. "The Monopolizing Woman Teacher." *Education Review* (Jan. 1912):

17-40. Print.

Berlin, James. *Rhetoric and Reality: Writing Instruction in American Colleges, 1900-1985*. Carbondale: Southern Illinois UP, 1987. Print.

———. *Writing Instruction in Nineteenth-Century American Colleges*. Carbondale: Southern Illinois UP, 1984. Print.

Biesecker, Barbara. "Of Historicity, Rhetoric: The Archive as Scene of Invention." *Rhetoric and Public Affairs* 9.1 (2006): 124-31. Print.

Brereton, John, ed. *The Origins of Composition Studies in the American College, 1875-1925*. Pittsburgh: U of Pittsburgh P, 1995. Print.

Connors, Robert. *Composition-Rhetoric: Backgrounds, Theory, and Pedagogy*. Pittsburgh: U of Pittsburgh P, 1997. Print.

———. "Dreams and Play: Historical Method and Methodology." *Selected Essays of Robert J. Connors*. Ed. Lisa Ede and Andrea Lunsford. Boston: Bedford/St. Martin's, 2003. 221-35. Print.

Cortés, Carlos. "The Mexican American Press." *The Ethnic Press in the United States*. Ed. Sally M. Miller. New York: Greenwood, 1987. 247-60. Print.

Crowley, Sharon. *Composition in the University: Historical and Polemical Essays*. Pittsburgh: U of Pittsburgh P, 1998. Print.

Donahue, Patricia, and Gretchen Fletcher Moon, eds. *Local Histories: Reading the Archives of Composition*. Pittsburgh: U of Pittsburgh P, 2007. Print.

Enoch, Jessica. "*Para la Mujer:* Defining a Chicana Feminist Rhetoric at the Turn of the Century." *College English* 67.1 (2003): 20-37. Print.

———. *Refiguring Rhetorical Education: Women Teaching African American, Native American, and Chicano/a Students, 1865-1911*. Carbondale: Southern Illinois UP, 2008. Print.

Ferreira-Buckley, Linda. "Rescuing the Archives from Foucault." *College English* 61.5 (1999): 577-83. Print.

Foss, Karen A., Sonja K. Foss, and Cindy F. Griffin. *Feminist Rhetorical Theories*. London: Sage, 1999. Print.

Gaillet, Lynée Lewis. "Archival Survival: Navigating Historical Research." Ramsey et al. 28-39.

Gere, Anne Ruggles. "Kitchen Tables and Rented Rooms: The Extracurriculum of Composition." *CCC* 45.1 (1994): 75-107. Print.

———. *Intimate Practices: Literacy and Cultural Work in U.S. Women's Clubs, 1880-1920*. Urbana: U of Illinois P, 1997. Print.

Glenn, Cheryl, and Jessica Enoch. "Drama in the Archives: Re-Reading Materials, Re-Writing History." *CCC* 61.2 (2009): 321-42. Print.

Gold, David. "The Accidental Archivist: Embracing Chance and Confusion in Historical Scholarship." *Beyond the Archives: Research as a Lived Process*. Ed. Gesa Kirsch and Liz Rohan. Carbondale: Southern Illinois UP, 2008. 13-19. Print.

———. *Rhetoric at the Margins: Revising the History of Writing Instruction in American Colleges, 1873-1947*. Carbondale: Southern Illinois UP, 2008. Print.

Gutiérrez, Félix. "Spanish-Language Media in America: Background, Resources, History." *Journalism History* 4.2 (Summer 1977): 34-41, 65-67. Print.

Gutiérrez, Ramón A. "The UCLA Bibliographic Survey of Mexican American Literary Culture, 1821-1945: An Overview." *Recovering the U.S. Hispanic Literary Heritage*. Ed. Ramón Gutiérrez and Genaro Padilla. Houston: Arte Público, 1993. 309-14. Print.

"Heritage Foundation Slates Photo Exhibit Opening of 'Reading, 'Riting and Revolution—The Kindergarten Students of Leonor Villegas Magnon.'" *Laredo Morning Times* (1 March 1998): 6D. Print.

"Heritage Foundation Declares 'S.O.S.' (Save Our Story) Campaign." *Heritage Register* (Summer 2000): 8. Print.

Horner, Bruce, and John Trimbur. "English Only and College Composition." *CCC* 53.4 (2002): 594-630. Print.

Idar, Jovita. "The Mexican Children in Texas." Trans. Jess Enoch, Lisa Lawson, and Raquel Moran Tellez. *La Crónica* 3.32 (10 Aug. 1911): 1. Print.

Jarratt, Susan. "Classics and Counterpublics in Nineteenth-Century Historically Black Colleges." *College English* 72.2 (2009): 134-59. Print.

"Jovita Idea [sic] (1885-1946)." *Laredo Morning Times* (6 Sept. 1992): 8D. Print.

Kates, Susan. *Activist Rhetorics and American Higher Education, 1885-1937*. Carbondale: Southern Illinois UP, 2001. Print.

Kirsch, Gesa, and Liz Rohan, eds. *Beyond the Archives: Research as a Lived Process*. Carbondale: Southern Illinois UP, 2008. Print.

Kirsch, Gesa, and Patricia Sullivan. "Introduction." *Methods and Methodology in Composition Research*. Ed. Gesa Kirsch and Patricia Sullivan. Carbondale: Southern Illinois UP, 1992. 1-11. Print.

Kirsch, Gesa. "Being on Location: Serendipity, Place, and Archival Research." *Beyond the Archives: Research as a Lived Process*. Ed. Gesa Kirsch and Liz Rohan. Carbondale: Southern Illinois UP, 2008. 20-27. Print.

Kitzhaber, Albert. *Rhetoric in the American Colleges, 1850-1900*. Dallas: Southern Methodist UP, 1990. Print.

L'Eplattenier, Barbara. "Opinion: Archival Research Methods." *College English* 72.1 (2009): 67-79. Print.

———. "Questioning our Methodological Metaphors." *Calling Cards: Theory and Practice in the Study of Race, Gender, and Culture*. Ed. Jacqueline Jones Royster and Ann Marie Simpkins. Albany: SUNY P, 2005. 133-146. Print.

"Leonor Villegas de Magnon, Hero of the Mexican Revolution." *Laredo Morning Times* (30 Aug. 1992): 5D. Print.

Limón, José. "*El Primer Congreso Mexicanista de 1911*: A Precursor to Contemporary Chicanismo." *Aztlán* 5:1-2 (1974): 85-117. Print.

Logan, Shirley Wilson. "Introduction: Mounting the Platform." *With Pen and Voice: A Critical Anthology of Nineteenth-Century African American Women*. Ed. Shirley Wilson Logan. Carbondale: Southern Illinois UP, 1995. Print.

———. *Liberating Language: Sites of Rhetorical Education in Nineteenth-Century Black America*. Carbondale: Southern Illinois UP, 2008. Print.

Matsuda, Paul. "The Myth of Linguistic Homogeneity in U.S. College Composition." *College English* 68.6 (2006): 637-51. Print.

Meyer, Doris. "Reading Early Neomexicano Newspapers: Yesterday and Today." *Recovering the U.S. Hispanic Literary Heritage*. Ed. Maria Herrera-Sobek and Virginia Sánchez-Korrol. Vol. 3. Houston: Arte Público, 2000. 402-11. Print.

Morris, Charles E. "The Archival Turn in Rhetorical Studies; Or, The Archive's Rhetorical (Re)turn." *Rhetoric and Public Affairs* 9.1 (2006): 113-52. Print.

Morris, Sammie, and Shirley Rose. "Invisible Hands: Recognizing Archivists' Work to Make Records Accessible." Ramsey et al. 51-78.

Murphy, James. "Prologue: The Politics of Historiography." *Rhetoric Review* 7.1

(1988): 5-6. Print.

Nunley, Vorris. "From the Hush Harbor to Da Academic Hood: Hush Harbors and an African American Rhetorical Tradition." *African American Rhetoric(s): Interdisciplinary Perspectives*. Ed. Elaine Richardson and Ronald Jackson II. Carbondale: Southern Illinois UP, 2004. 221-41. Print.

"Octalog: The Politics of Historiography." *Rhetoric Review* 6.2 (1988): 5-49. Print.

"Octalog II: The (Continuing) Politics of Historiography." *Rhetoric Review* 16.1 (1997): 22-44. Print.

Ramírez, Cristina D. "Forging a Mestiza Rhetoric: Mexican Women Journalists' Role in the Construction of a National Identity." *College English* 71.6 (2009): 606-29. Print.

Ramsey, Alexis, et al., eds. *Working in the Archives: Practical Research Methods for Rhetoric and Composition*. Carbondale: Southern Illinois UP, 2010. Print.

Ritter, Kelly. *Before Shaughnessy: Basic Writing at Yale and Harvard, 1920-1960*. Carbondale: Southern Illinois UP, 2009. Print.

Reynolds, Nedra. *Geographies of Writing: Inhabiting Places and Encountering Difference*. Carbondale: Southern Illinois UP, 2004. Print.

Rodriguez, América. *Making Latino News: Race, Language, Class*. London: Sage, 1999. Print.

Romano, Susan. "Tlaltelolco: The Grammatical-Rhetorical *Indios* of Colonial Mexico." *College English* 66.3 (2004): 257-77. Print.

Royster, Jacqueline Jones, and Jean C. Williams. "History and the Spaces Left: African American Presence and Narratives of Composition Studies." *CCC* 50.4 (1999): 563-84. Print.

Royster, Jacqueline Jones. *Traces of a Stream: Literacy and Social Change Among African American Women*. Pittsburgh: U of Pittsburgh P, 2000. Print.

San Miguel Jr., Guadalupe. *"Let Them All Take Heed": Mexican Americans and the Campaign for Educational Equality in Texas, 1910-1981*. Austin: U of Texas P, 1987. Print.

Schneider, Stephen. "Freedom Schooling: Stokely Carmichael and Critical Rhetorical Education." *CCC* 58.1 (2006): 46-69. Print.

Schultz, Lucille. *Young Composers: Composition's Beginnings in the Nineteenth Century*. Carbondale: Southern Illinois UP, 1999. Print.

Sharer, Wendy. "Disintegrating Bodies of Knowledge: Historical Material and Revisionary Histories of Rhetoric." *Rhetorical Bodies*. Ed. Jack Selzer and Sharon Crowley. Madison: U of Wisconsin P, 1999. 120-39. Print.

Steward, Doug. "The Foreign Language Requirement in English Doctoral Programs." *Profession* (2006): 203-18. Print.

Sutherland, Christine Mason. "Getting to Know Them: Concerning Research into Four Early Women Writers." Kirsch and Rohan 28-36.

Tirabassi, Katherine. "Journeying into the Archives: Exploring the Pragmatics of Archival Research." Ramsey et al. 169-180.

Vitanza, Victor, ed. *Writing Histories of Rhetoric*. Carbondale: Southern Illinois UP, 1994. Print.

Warnick, Chris. "Locating the Archives: Finding Aids and Archival Scholarship in Composition and Rhetoric." Ramsey et al. 91-101.

Weidner, Heidemarie Z. "A Chair 'Perpetually Filled by a Female Professor': Rhetoric and Composition Instruction at Nineteenth-Century Butler University."

Donahue and Moon 58-76.

Zavella, Patricia. "Reflections on Diversity among Chicanas." *Frontiers* 12.2 (1999): 73-85.

Zenger, Amy. "Race, Composition, and 'Our English': Performing the Mother Tongue in a Daily Theme Assignment at Harvard." *Rhetoric Review* 23.4 (2004): 332-49. Print.

Appendix: Historiographic Locations

Bacon, Jacqueline, and Glen McClish. "Reinventing the Master's Tools: Nineteenth-Century African-American Literary Societies of Philadelphia and Rhetorical Education." *Rhetoric Society Quarterly* 30.4 (2000): 19-47. Print.
  *Philadelphia, PA 19104

Berlin, James. *Rhetoric and Reality: Writing Instruction in American Colleges, 1900-1985*. Carbondale: Southern Illinois UP, 1987. Print.
  *Harvard U: Cambridge, MA 02139
  *Columbia U: New York, NY 10019
  *U of Texas: Austin, TX 78701
  *U of Illinois: Urbana, IL 61801
  *U of Wisconsin: Madison, WI 53701
  *Yale U: New Haven, CT 06510
  *Princeton U: Princeton, NJ 08544
  *Williams College: Williamstown, MA 01267
  *U of Michigan: Ann Arbor, MI 48109

———. *Writing Instruction in Nineteenth-Century American Colleges*. Carbondale: Southern Illinois UP, 1984. Print.
  *Harvard U: Cambridge, MA 02139
  *Yale U: New Haven, CT 06510
  *Amherst College: Amherst, MA 01003
  * U of Michigan: Ann Arbor, MI 48109

Brereton, John, ed. *The Origins of Composition Studies in the American College, 1875-1925*. Pittsburgh: U of Pittsburgh P, 1995. Print.
  *Harvard U: Cambridge, MA 02139
  *Yale U: New Haven, CT 06510
  *Stanford U: Stanford, CA 94305
  *U of Iowa: Iowa City, IA 52242-7700
  *Indiana U: Bloomington, IN 47405-7000
  *Amherst College: Amherst, MA 01003
  *U of Michigan: Ann Arbor, MI 48109
  *U of Nebraska: Lincoln, NE 68588
  *U of Pennsylvania: Philadelphia, PA 19104
  *Wellesley College: Wellesley, MA 02481
  *U of Minnesota: Minneapolis, MN 55455

Campbell, JoAnn. "Controlling Voices: The Legacy of English A at Radcliffe College, 1883-1917." *CCC* 43.4 (1992): 472-85. Print.
  *Radcliffe College: Cambridge, MA 02139

———. "Freshman (*sic*) English: A Nineteenth-Century Wellesley 'Girl' Negotiates Authority." *Rhetoric Review* 15.1 (1996): 110-27. Print.

* Wellesley College: Wellesley, MA 02481
———. "'A Real Vexation': Student Writing in Mount Holyoke's Culture of Service, 1837-1865." *College English* 59.7 (1997): 767-88. Print.
*Mount Holyoke: South Hadley, MA 01075
———, ed. *Toward a Feminist Rhetoric: The Writing of Gertrude Buck*. Pittsburgh: U of Pittsburgh P, 1996. Print.
*U of Michigan: Ann Arbor, MI 48109
Clark, Gregory. "The Oratorical Poetic of Timothy Dwight." *Oratorical Culture in Nineteenth-Century America: Transformations in the Theory and Practice of Rhetoric*. Carbondale: Southern Illinois UP, 1993. 57-77. Print.
*Yale U: New Haven, CT 06510
Corbett, Edward P.J. "The Cornell School of Rhetoric." *Rhetoric Review* 4.1 (1985): 4-14. Print.
*Cornell U: Ithaca, NY 14853
Crowley, Sharon. *Composition in the University: Historical and Polemical Essays*. Pittsburgh: U of Pittsburgh P, 1998. Print.
*U of Iowa: Iowa City, IA 52242-7700
*Harvard U: Cambridge, MA 02139
*Yale U: New Haven, CT 06510
*Princeton U: Princeton, NJ 08544
*U of Michigan: Ann Arbor, MI 48109
———. "Invention in Nineteenth-Century Rhetoric." *CCC* 36.1 (1985): 51-60. Print.
*Harvard U: Cambridge, MA 02139
*Amherst College: Amherst, MA 01003
DeGenaro, William. "William Rainey Harper and the Ideology of Service at Junior Colleges." Donahue and Moon 181-198.
*Joliet Junior College: Joliet, IL 60432
DePalma, Michael-John. "Austin Phelps and the Spirit (of) Composing: An Exploration of Nineteenth Century Sacred Rhetoric at Andover Theological Seminary." *Rhetoric Review* 27.4 (2008): 379-76. Print.
*Andover Theological Seminary: Andover, MA 01810
Desser, Daphne. "Fraught Literacy: American Missionary Women in Nineteenth-Century Hawai'i." *College English* 69.5 (2007): 443-469. Print.
*Captain Cook, HI 96704
Donahue, Patricia, and Bianca Falbo. "(The Teaching of) Reading and Writing at Lafayette College." Donahue and Moon 38-57.
*Lafayette College: Easton, PA 18042
Douglas, Wallace. "Rhetoric for the Meritocracy: The Creation of Composition at Harvard." *English in America*. Ed. Richard Ohmann. Hanover: Wesleyan UP, 1976. 97-132. Print.
*Harvard U: Cambridge, MA 02139
Enoch, Jessica. *Refiguring Rhetorical Education: Women Teaching African American, Native American, and Chicano/a Students*. Southern Illinois UP, 2008. Print.
*Carlisle, PA 17013
*Laredo, TX 78040
Fitzgerald, Kathryn. "The Platteville Papers Revisited: Gender and Genre in a Normal School Writing Assignment." Donahue and Moon 115-133.

68 *Composition Studies*

*Platteville, WI 53818-3099

Garbus, Julie. "Vida Scudder in the Classroom and in the Archives." Donahue and Moon 77-93.
*Wellesley College: Wellesley, MA 02481

Gleason, Barbara. "Remediation Phase-Out at CUNY: The 'Equity versus Excellence' Controversy." *CCC* 51.3 (2000): 488-452. Print.
*City U of New York: New York, NY 10019

Gold, David. *Rhetoric at the Margins: Revising the History of Writing Instruction in American Colleges, 1873-1947*. Carbondale: Southern Illinois UP, 2008. Print.
*Texas Woman's U: Denton, TX 76204
*Wiley College: Marshall, TX 75670
*East Texas Normal College: Commerce, TX 75428

Gray, Patrice. "Life in the Margins: Student Writing and Curricular Change at Fitchburg Normal, 1895-1910." Donahue and Moon 159-180.
*Fitchburg Normal College: Fitchburg, MA 01420

Greer, Jane. "'No Smiling Madonna': Marion Wharton and the Struggle to Construct a Critical Pedagogy for the Working Class, 1914-1917." *CCC* 51.2 (1999): 248-71. Print.
*People's College: Fort Scott, KS 66701

Harmon, Sandra D. "'The Voice, Pen and Influence of Our Women Are Abroad in the Land': Women and the Illinois State Normal University." *Nineteenth-Century Women Learn to Write*. Ed. Catherine Hobbs. Charlottesville: U of Virginia P, 1995. 84-102. Print.
*Illinois State Normal U: Normal, IL 61790

Hirst, Russell. "The Sermon as Public Discourse: Austin Phelps and the Conservative Homiletic Tradition in Nineteenth-Century America." *Oratorical Culture in Nineteenth-Century America: Transformations in the Theory and Practice of Rhetoric*. Carbondale: Southern Illinois UP, 1993. 78-109. Print.
*Andover Theological Seminary: Andover, MA 01810

Hollis, Karyn L. *Liberating Voices: Writing at the Bryn Mawr Summer School for Women Workers*. Carbondale: Southern Illinois UP, 2004. Print.
* Bryn Mawr College: Bryn Mawr, PA 19010

Hoogeveen, Jeffrey L. "The Progressive Faculty/Student Discourse of 1969-1970 and the Emergence of Lincoln University's Writing Program." Donahue and Moon 199-219.
* Lincoln U: Lincoln, PA 19352

Jarratt, Susan. "Classics and Counterpublics in Nineteenth-Century Historically Black Colleges." *College English* 72.2 (2009): 134-59. Print.
*Fisk U: Nashville, TN 37208
*Atlanta U: Atlanta, GA 30301
*Howard U: Washington DC 20059

Johnson, Nan. "Rhetoric and Belles Lettres in the Canadian Academy: An Historical Analysis." *College English* 50.8 (1988): 861-73. Print.
*U of Toronto: Toronto, ON, Canada M4B 1B3
*Dalhousie U: Halifax, NS, Canada B3H 4R2
*McGill U: Montreal, QC, Canada H3A 2T5

Jolliffe, David A. "The Moral Subject in College Composition: A Conceptual Framework and the Case of Harvard, 1865-1900." *College English* 51.2 (1989):

163-73. Print.
    *Harvard U: Cambridge, MA 02139
Kates, Susan. *Activist Rhetorics and American Higher Education, 1885-1937*. Carbondale: Southern Illinois UP, 2001. Print.
    *Smith College: Northampton, MA 01060
    *Wilberforce College: Wilberforce, OH 45384-1001
    *Brookwood Labor College: Katonah, NY 10536
———. "Literacy, Voting Rights, and the Citizenship Schools in the South, 1957-1970." *CCC* 57.3 (2006): 479-502. Print.
    *Monteagle, TN 37356
Kitzhaber, Albert. *Rhetoric in American Colleges, 1850-1900*. Dallas: Southern Methodist UP, 1990. Print.
    *Harvard U: Cambridge, MA 02139
    *Yale U: New Haven, CT 06510
    *U of Michigan: Ann Arbor, MI 48109
    *Amherst College: Amherst, MA 01003
Larsen, Elizabeth. "The Progress of Literacy: Edward Tyrrel Channing and the Separation of the Student Writer from the World." *Rhetoric Review* 11.1 (1992): 159-71. Print.
    *Harvard U: Cambridge, MA 02139
Lerner, Neal. "Rejecting the Remedial Brand: The Rise and Fall of the Dartmouth Writing Clinic." *CCC* 59.1 (2007): 13-35. Print.
    *Dartmouth U: Hanover, NH 03755
Lindblom, Kenneth, William Banks, and Risë Quay. "Mid-Nineteenth Century Writing Instruction at Illinois State University." Donahue and Moon 94-114.
    * Illinois State U: Normal, IL 61790
Lindbloom, Kenneth, and Patricia A. Dunn. "Cooperative Writing 'Program' Administration at Illinois State University: The Committee on English of 1904-05 and the Influence of Professor J. Rose Colby." *Historical Studies of Writing Program Administration: Individuals, Communities, and the Formation of a Discipline*. Ed. Barbara L'Eplattenier and Lisa Mastrangelo. West Lafayette: Parlor, 2004. 37-70. Print.
    *Illinois State U: Normal, IL 61790
Martin, Harold. "Freshman Composition: Harvard Beginnings." *CCC* 13.3 (1962): 35-36. Print.
    *Harvard U: Cambridge, MA 02139
Mastrangelo, Lisa S. "The Grand Narrative of Fred Newton Scott." *College English* 72.3 (2010): 248-68. Print.
    *U of Michigan: Ann Arbor, MI 48109
———. "Learning From the Past: Rhetoric, Composition, and Debate at Mount Holyoke College." *Rhetoric Review* 18.1 (1999): 46-64. Print.
    *Mount Holyoke College: South Hadley, MA 01075
Mihesuah, Devon A. "'Let Us Strive Earnestly to Value Education Aright': Cherokee Female Seminarians as Leaders of a Changing Culture." *Nineteenth-Century Women Learn to Write*. Ed. Catherine Hobbs. Charlottesville: U of Virginia P, 1995. 103-119. Print.
    *Tahlequah, OK 74464
Newkirk, Thomas. "The Politics of Intimacy: The Defeat of Barrett Wendell at

Harvard." *Taking Stock: The Writing Process Movement in the '90s*. Portsmouth: Boynton/Cook, 1994. 115-32. Print.

    *Harvard U: Cambridge, MA 02139

Paine, Charles. *The Resistant Writer: Rhetoric as Immunity, 1850 to the Present*. Albany: SUNY P, 1999. Print.

    *Harvard U: Cambridge, MA 02139 (Channing)

    *Harvard U: Cambridge, MA 02139 (Hill)

Reid, Ronald F. "Edward Everett and Neoclassical Oratory in Genteel America." *Oratorical Culture in Nineteenth-Century America: Transformations in the Theory and Practice of Rhetoric*. Carbondale: Southern Illinois UP, 1993. 29-56. Print.

    *Harvard U: Cambridge, MA 02139

Ricks, Vickie. "'In an Atmosphere of Peril': College Women and Their Writing." *Nineteenth-Century Women Learn to Write*. Ed. Catherine Hobbs. Charlottesville: U of Virginia P, 1995. 59-83. Print.

    *Vassar College: Poughkeepsie, NY 12604

Ritter, Kelly. "Before Mina Shaughnessy: Basic Writing at Yale, 1920-1960." *CCC* 60.1 (2008): 12-45. Print.

    *Yale U: New Haven, CT 06510

Romano, Susan. "Tlaltelolco: The Grammatical-Rhetorical *Indios* of Colonial Mexico." *College English* 66.3 (2004): 257-77. Print.

    *Tlaltelolco, México, D.F. 06995

Rothermel, Beth Ann. "'Our Life's Work': Rhetorical Preparation and Teacher Training at a Massachusetts State Normal School, 1839-1929." Donahue and Moon 134-158.

    *Westfield State Normal School: Westfield, MA 01086-1630

Russell, David. *Writing in the Academic Disciplines, 1870-1990: A Curricular History*. Carbondale: Southern Illinois UP, 1991. Print.

    *Colgate U: Hamilton, NY 13346

    *U of California at Berkeley: Berkeley, CA 94720

    *Iowa State U: Ames, IA 50011

    *Harvard U: Cambridge, MA 02139

    *Columbia U: New York, NY 10019

    *U of Chicago: Chicago, IL 60637

    *U of Kansas: Lawrence, KS 66045

    *U of Missouri: Columbia, MO 65211

    *U of Michigan: Ann Arbor, MI 48109

    *U of Minnesota: Minneapolis, MN 55455

    *Ohio State U: Columbus, OH 43210

    *MIT: Cambridge, MA 02139

    *Central College: Pella, IA 50219

    *Radcliffe College: Cambridge, MA 02139

Simmons, Sue Carter. "Constructing Writers: Barrett Wendell's Pedagogy at Harvard." *CCC* 46.3 (1995): 327-352. Print.

    *Harvard U: Cambridge, MA 02139

———. "Radcliffe Responds to Harvard Rhetoric: 'An Absurdly Stiff Way of Thinking'." *Nineteenth-Century Women Learn to Write*. Ed. Catherine Hobbs. Charlottesville: U of Virginia P, 1995. 264-292. Print.

*Radcliffe College: Cambridge, MA 02139

Schneider, Stephen. "Freedom Schooling: Stokely Carmichael and Critical Rhetorical Education." *CCC* 58.1 (2006): 46-69. Print.
    *Waveland, MS 39576

Scott, Blake. "John Witherspoon's Normalizing Pedagogy of Ethos." *Rhetoric Review* 16.1 (1997): 58-75. Print.
    *Princeton U: Princeton, NJ 08544

Scott, Patrick. "Jonathan Maxcy and the Aims of Early Nineteenth-Century Rhetorical Teaching." *College English* 45.1 (1983): 21-30. Print.
    *U of South Carolina: Columbia, SC 29208

Soliday, Mary. *The Politics of Remediation: Institutional and Student Needs in Higher Education*. Pittsburgh: U of Pittsburgh P, 2002. Print.
    *City U of New York: New York, NY 10019

Spring, Suzanne B. "'Seemingly Uncouth Forms': Letters at Mount Holyoke Female Seminary." *CCC* 59.4 (2008): 633-75. Print.
    *Mount Holyoke U: South Hadley, MA 01075

Stewart, Donald. "Harvard's Influence on English Studies: Perceptions from Three Universities in the Early Twentieth Century." *CCC* 43 (1992): 455-71. Print.
    *Harvard U: Cambridge, MA 02139
    *Michigan U: Ann Arbor, MI 48109
    *Cornell U: Ithaca, NY 14853
    *Columbia U: New York, NY 10019

———. "Two Model Teachers and the Harvardization of English Departments." *The Rhetorical Tradition and Modern Writing*. Ed. James Murphy. New York: MLA, 1982. Print.
    *Harvard U: Cambridge, MA 02139 (Child)
    *U of Michigan: Ann Arbor, MI 48109

Stewart, Donald C., and Patricia L. Stewart. *The Life and Legacy of Fred Newton Scott*. Pittsburgh: U of Pittsburgh P, 1997. Print.
    *U of Michigan: Ann Arbor, MI 48109

Varnum, Robin. *Fencing with Words: A History of Writing Instruction at Amherst College During the Era of Theodore Baird, 1938-1966*. Urbana: NCTE, 1996. Print.
    *Amherst College: Amherst, MA 01003

Weidner, Heidemarie Z. "A Chair 'Perpetually Filled by a Female Professor': Rhetoric and Composition Instruction at Nineteenth-Century Butler University." Donahue and Moon 58-76.
    *Butler U: Indianapolis, IN 46208

Welch, Kathleen. "Thinking Like *That*: The Ideal Nineteenth-Century Student Writer." Donahue and Moon 14-37.
    *Oberlin College: Oberlin, OH 44074

Wells, Susan. *Out of the Dead House: Nineteenth-Century Women Physicians and the Writing of Medicine*. Madison: U of Wisconsin, 2001. Print.
    *Philadelphia, PA 19104

Wible, Scott. "Pedagogies of the 'Students' Right' Era: The Language Curriculum Research Group's Project for Linguistic Diversity." *CCC* 57.3 (February 2006): 442-78. Print.
    *Brooklyn College: New York, NY 10019

———. "Professor Burke's Bennington Project." *Rhetoric Society Quarterly* 38.3 (2008): 259-82. Print.

    *Bennington College: Bennington, VT 05201

Westbrook, B. Evelyn. "Debating Both Sides: What Nineteenth-Century College Debating Societies Can Teach Us about Critical Pedagogy." *Rhetoric Review* 21.4 (2002): 339-56. Print.

    *U of South Carolina: Columbia, SC 29208

Whitburn, Merrill D. "Rhetorical Theory in Yale's Graduate School in the Late Nineteenth Century: The Example of William C. Robinson's Forensic Oratory." *Rhetoric Society Quarterly* 34.4 (2004): 55-70. Print.

    *Yale U: New Haven, CT 06510

Zaluda, Scott. "Lost Voices of the Harlem Renaissance: Writing Assigned at Howard University, 1919-31." *CCC* 50.2 (1998): 232-48. Print.

    *Howard U: Washington, DC 20059

Zenger, Amy. "Race, Composition, and 'Our English': Performing the Mother Tongue in a Daily Theme Assignment at Harvard." *Rhetoric Review* 23.4 (2004): 332-49. Print.

    *Harvard U: Cambridge, MA 02139

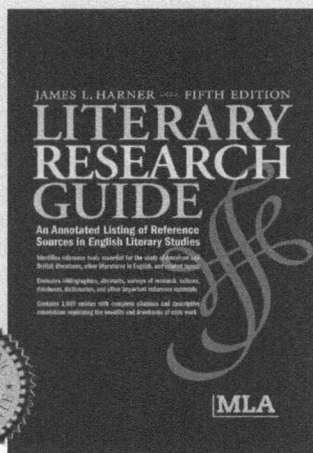

Podcasting and Performativity: Multimodal Invention in an Advanced Writing Class

Leigh A. Jones

This article points composition scholars toward two bodies of theory that are gaining attention in our discipline, performance studies and multi-modal discourse theory. Each raises important questions about the ways we teach writing, the kinds of composition processes we value, and the means by which students construct authority in the university. The author argues that by combining performance studies and multimodal discourse theories with invention strategies early in the research writing process, instructors can enhance the effectiveness of students struggling to adopt an authoritative voice in research papers. Instructors can merge these approaches productively by assigning student-generated podcasts.

In an age of (multi)media, we can no longer ignore the embodied nature of discourse, and we are having to rethink almost every aspect of the teaching of writing, from ways of being in the classroom to the kinds of assignments students do and how those assignments are delivered and assessed. For us, the notion of performance is crucial to participating in this work.
   —Jenn Fishman et al., "Performing Writing, Performing Literacy"
      (229)

By broadening the choice of composing modalities, I argue we expand the field of play for students with different learning styles and different ways of reflecting on the world; we provide the opportunity for them to study, think critically about, and work with new communicative modes. Such a move not only offers us a chance to make instruction increasingly effective for those students from different cultural and linguistic backgrounds, but it also provides an opportunity to make our work increasingly relevant to a changing set of communicative needs in a globalized world.
   —Cynthia L. Selfe, "The Movement of Air, the Breath of Meaning"
      (644)

Most who have taught or taken a composition class would agree: the classroom is disorienting for everyone involved—students and instructors. We are trying to figure each other out, assessing our audience, stepping into new mental and physical space, performing in new ways. At the urban university where I teach a junior-level writing class, this disorientation is nuanced by each student who attends and each writing instructor who works to help students write more effectively as they negotiate their way. My students' writing insecurities are like those of most college students in many ways. Like all students, theirs include a fear of taking independent risks in writing. My students' fears are reflected in research on traditional students at highly selective universities. Fishman et al. found that while students at Stanford University were risk-takers in their writing outside of class, their initial confidence as academic writers waned significantly by the end of the first year (231).[1] Of course, risks are required for academic productivity and creativity—whatever goals students and instructors may have for students' growth as writers. Writing is a transformative process in that it requires us to imagine our audiences and ourselves anew, and this productive and creative transformation is inherently risky, particularly when evaluated by an experienced audience. Bravery in writing, what I call risk-taking, has been attributed to past positive experiences (Fishman et al. 232).[2] I look for ways to encourage this risk-taking by drawing from my students' positive experiences and strengths, attempting to make their risky invention process more productive and their writing process more transformative. Students' positive experiences and strengths typically include a high level of ease and skill at talking in class about their research topics, demonstrating an engagement with research and analysis that is not reflected in the papers they write. Their strong analysis and research skills do not convince them that they can produce a successful academic research paper.

Recently, I decided to take a risk myself and try something new at the beginning of an advanced writing course: podcasting. While podcasting has become a popular project for students at the end of a semester, I wondered how it would work as a prelude to drafting rather than a presentation of their finished work. And as I sat in class listening to the podcasts my students eventually produced early that semester, I was surprised by what happened. Students jumped into the assignment, took creative risks—the kind they feared with writing assignments—and seemed to enjoy doing so. Not only did students enjoy the podcasting, but as they proceeded through the drafting process of their research papers, they formed useful workshop groups in which they became invested in their own and each other's work. Over the course of the class, they talked more freely about their writing, and they ultimately produced more authoritative, sophisticated writing, taking ownership over their academic voices and earning higher grades than students in the same course during prior semesters. Making the initial risk-taking production an aural performance rather than a paper draft seemed to benefit students. It was one of those moments writing instructors hope for. And it happened again the next semester.

For example, one student, "V,"[3] chose to create his podcast under the guise of a radio talk show host interviewing a guest about his research topic Here's an excerpt of V's podcast script that demonstrates how he used the exercise to articulate a nascent research question:

AJ: *Welcome everyone. This is AJ, your talk show host for tonight. The presidential debates are heating up and free trade is one of the hottest topics right now. To discuss the issue, we have with us V, representative of investment corporations. Welcome to the show, Mr. V.*

V: *Thank you, AJ.*

AJ: *So, free trade has given corporations an unwarranted reason to outsource jobs in order to maximize their own profit, while our American workers are left unemployed. So why should we practice free trade?*

As writing and rhetoric instructors search for ways to meet the varying needs of student writers along the sequence of courses from first-year composition to senior-level courses and beyond, we are increasingly turning to multimodal learning and discourse as a way to place writing into a contemporary context outside of the academic setting. In her recent *CCC* article "The Movement of Air, the Breath of Meaning: Aurality and Multimodal Composing," Cynthia L. Selfe calls on compositionists to think beyond our historical academic focus on written communication over aural. This history, she argues, "functions to limit our professional understanding of composing as a multimodal rhetorical activity and deprives students of valuable semiotic resources for making meaning" (617). In this article I focus on the performative, semiotic element of aural composing, an element that I have found to benefit students early in their writing processes. Since the 1980s, composition scholars have understood via linguistics theory that the earlier dichotomy we constructed between speaking and writing was false (Selfe 628). Yet this informed understanding has not transformed classroom practices generally. Today, multimodal resources invite aurality into all educational spaces. Through multimodal performance, we find a means of mending the speaking/writing division that we have instituted in our pedagogical practices.

As a currently popular and widely advertised technology on many college campuses, podcasting offers the potential for exploring the aural mode of communication in service of the written. More specifically, podcasts offer important epistemological possibilities. One of the most useful possibilities for a writing class is that podcasts can help us address the rhetorical conventions of research-based learning and expression that we expect from student writers by connecting the writing process to performance. In his 2008 article "Performing/Teaching/Writing: Performance Studies in the Composition Classroom," Ryan Claycomb argues that while Composition Studies has begun to ask questions about how writing instructors can incorporate performance studies into our pedagogy, little work has been done on the subject. Performance studies draws from ideas about power, discourse, and public display that emerge from the theories of gender scholar Judith Butler, philosopher J.L. Austin, and literary critic Eve Kosofsky Sedgwick, among others. As a relatively new area of study that incorporates and influences disciplines including theater, dance, philosophy, gender studies, and English, and overlaps with cultural studies more generally, performance studies can help us understand on a theoretical and practical level how and why to incorporate digital technology into a writing-focused class. A guiding question for our pedagogy should be: In what ways could (what I call) a performative epistemology help students better use invention to their advantage in their writing, and how might technology, such as podcasting, enable this kind of epistemology?

Compositionists have been exploring this question in a variety of ways. My conversations with other writing faculty increasingly turn to multimodal discourse, which sometimes includes podcasting as a venue for student presentations at the end of a semester by incorporating performative elements and multimodality as a culmination of the writing process. This approach is becoming a popular way for instructors across the disciplines to experiment with digital audio and visual technology in their courses (Tremel and Jesson). By contrast, what I offer here is an exploration of the role podcasts might play as an epistemological tool in the invention process: that is to say, an epistemology that is employed before students begin drafting and one that continues to enhance students' rhetorical awareness throughout the recursive research-writing process. I will explore the performative elements involved, arguing that performativity in this classroom context can help alleviate the counter-productive anxiety that many students feel at the beginning of a writing class, even though they may have strong aural communication and critical thinking skills. I have observed this effect over two semesters of teaching with podcasts in an urban university comprised primarily of racially, ethnically, and linguistically non-traditional students. As writing teachers turn to podcasting in their writing classes to present lectures or require students to produce podcasts at the end of a project in lieu of oral presentations, they might also consider using podcasts at the beginning of a writing assignment as an epistemological strategy.

Invention, a term I use in this article to describe the beginning stage of a student's writing process, is one of the five departments of rhetoric into which ancient rhetoricians divided common rhetorical practices. For practitioners such as Aristotle, Cicero, and Quintillian, invention was the means to discover possible arguments. Aristotle categorized lines of argument according to four common topics: whether something is possible/impossible, did/did not occur, will/will not occur in the future, or whether it is better/worse or greater/lesser than something else (Lindemann 42). He also listed a second group of twenty-eight topics for creating arguments, such as arguments from definition and from cause and effect. Today, compositionists have generally interpreted *invention* as prewriting, including such activities as brainstorming, clustering, freewriting, journaling, and using heuristics, frameworks, and models for developing and organizing the arguments from which a writer will build an academic paper. However, these strategies can also be used at later stages in a writer's drafting process.

Podcasting is another tool that can help students to articulate and organize a paper topic as part of an invention process. And as with those strategies listed above, it could also be used during later stages of a student's writing process. Podcasting differs from written and visual methods of invention that I have listed above because it requires students to articulate their topic aloud, but more importantly, it is a public performance not solely for the writer and instructor's eyes. Role-playing exercises bear more resemblance to my podcasting activity in form and function; however, live role-playing does not allow students to re-record a performance until they deem it presentable for an audience. This process of re-recording the podcast, I argue, was especially important for my students, as it allowed them to think through the exercise and individually revise their performance as many times as they wanted to (for example, if they found that their presentation exceeded the time limit), and then to share their performance with students to receive feedback. Recording the podcast in solitude or with one partner also gave students more time and the creative autonomy to construct an authoritative persona, an element of the activity that I will visit later in this article.

I want to emphasize at the outset that I came to this teaching experience as an instructor who is not entirely at ease with technology, who did not own an mp3 player while I was learning to use mp3 files (podcasts) in the writing courses I taught, and who did not know how to create a podcast prior to the first semester I taught using them. I find podcasting to be an accessible pedagogical tool for writing instructors and students with a basic familiarity of online teaching environments like Blackboard.

Podcasting as a Performative Epistemology in the Writing Class

Much of the disorienting challenge of a writing classroom lies in its requirements as a performative space that is most often treated as natural in the moment: we perform as instructors, enacting the discourse of authority and student-teacher relationships; students perform as such, enacting their personae as learners, subordinates, subversives, and much less frequently, authorities (these are merely some of the many performances involved in any classroom); yet, we don't often recognize or confess these identities as performances. Such performance creates and validates a relationship among participants in the classroom, reifying through institutionalized ritual a discourse of power between teachers as authorities and students as recipients of knowledge. The paradox of this relationship is exposed when students are asked to perform as authoritative academic writers, a paradox that David Bartholomae made familiar in "Inventing the University": paraphrasing David Olsen, Bartholomae writes that

> the writer must learn that his authority is not established through his presence but through his absence—through his ability, that is, to speak as a god-like source beyond the limitations of any particular social or historical moment; to speak by means of the wisdom of convention through the oversounds of official or authoritative utterance, as the voice of logic or the voice of the community. (509)

Experienced writers know that they attain authority through rhetorical cues and conventions that adhere to contextual expectations. Student writers learn these cues at the same time that they perform their subordinate positions as students most literally through their physical presence as students. Peter McLaren pins down this nuanced, contradictory process more specifically as "enfleshment," a process of repetition, ritual, and habit that add up to a "dominant system of *lived* practices" (86). As Claycomb explains, through these practices, "teachers and students physically internalize the dominant power structures in the classroom" (6). Race, class, sexuality, and language become another layer that further defines the embodied roles students and instructors imagine and perform. Performing authority in writing under such conditions is made difficult because of the habitual performances in the physical classroom.

Selfe focuses on the role of speaking in this physical space, arguing that "the enactment of authority, power, and status in composition classes is expressed, in part, through aurality: how much one is allowed to talk and under what circumstances" (634). She historicizes the act of "silent writing, reading, and observation," by noting that it "became normalized [by the nineteenth century] and, importantly, linked to both class and race. [. . .] It was through such changes," she writes, "that writing became the focus of a specialized academic education delivered primarily to, and by, privileged white males" (623). Along with this shift, this silent authority of privileged white males characterized academic writing.

Often, students' insecurities manifest as a fear of taking the risk that is involved in beginning a lengthy research paper, and the invention process may not do enough to mitigate this fear. Such a process is enacted more easily when students have the belief that they can reach the end goal. Pretending to have authority through aural performance of a role is one way that my students developed this belief, shifting, to some degree, the power dynamics in the classroom by shifting the perception of who holds authority over subject matter. This shift works because we transformed the physical space of the classroom when everyone, including the instructor, became an audience for a student performance. Such embodiment of authority, what

Fishman et al. call "the act of embodying writing through voice, gesture, and movement," is part of an act of literacy (226). In the context of my advanced composition class, literacy meant the ability to analyze a sophisticated debate and make nuanced commentary about the role of argument, using a voice of academic authority.

College writing classes often overlook modes and qualities of expression such as theatricality that could lead to critical literacy, including deep rhetorical awareness of audience (Claycomb 5). They are, perhaps, practicing this deep rhetorical awareness in their extra-academic lives. As Meredith Love noted recently in her article on performativity, students are increasingly becoming aware of performance as a part of everyday activities. However, Kopelson laments, "Performativity remains most conspicuously absent, perhaps, from composition scholarship that is expressly pedagogical in focus" (qtd. in Love 15). Such performance could potentiate critical pedagogy. "Indeed," writes Ryan Claycomb,

> when we integrate elements of embodied performance into a Freirian problem-posing framework, a pedagogy that might otherwise conceive of critique in abstract terms takes significant steps toward a praxis that moves beyond the classroom space and into the lived experience of students and teachers. (2)

By drawing from students' lived experiences using performance, an activity such as podcasting allows students to enact an authoritative voice that potentially carries over into the performance of writing. While students adopted an authoritative voice as part of a role, they also became authorities—they came to understand that being an authority involves imagining one's self as an authority, whether they are communicating in writing or aurally, whether through prepared presentations or in more casual discussions about their topic during workshops or conferences with me. They came to know more about their topics than any other class member, including me, and we became an auxiliary part of this authority when we listened collectively to the podcasts, performing as an audience. Through their performance of an authoritative role, students were able to practice asserting themselves actively in the class. Rather than perpetuating the traditional discursive exchange between the students and the instructor, the podcasting performance disrupted the space of the class and made us all audience members. Along with this shift in authority, there was also an element of creative ownership, or perhaps even subversion, which took place during the podcasting assignment. If you look at the assignment description in the Appendix, you'll see that I asked students to begin their podcasts with the phrase "This just in . . ." However, many students (including V) chose to begin their podcasts differently. They interpreted the performance in new, productive ways, assuming creative authority over their projects.

Performance allows one to pass through a variety of roles. This act of inhabiting new spaces in the context of a writing class can allow students to "try on" authority in a productive way, as in the context of the podcasting assignment. And through doing so, students learn to use ethos to imagine their relationship to their audience and to appreciate the construction of knowledge through writing in new ways. In this sense, we can think of performance in relation to writing assignments as a performative epistemology. Schechner argues that performance requires us to "consider things as provisional, in-process, existing and changing over time, in rehearsal, as it were" (qtd. in Love 14). In the context of writing, students who use performance as part of the writing process come to understand their ethos as provisional, in process, and in rehearsal, a continual "trying on" and enacting. I don't mean to suggest that identity is absolutely fluid or that a writer can transcend socially-constructed and materially-experienced identities, but because identity isn't fixed, students can explore the authority that is available to them when they assume a new role.

In the podcast assignment, students were directed to perform a role that I defined, but they had the freedom to develop that role. Because students could re-record their podcasts as many times as they wanted before we listened to them as a class, they could experiment with different voices and rhetorical effects until they were happy with the recording. While some students chose to talk as if they were giving a report rather than taking on a more obviously dramatic role, the act of recording the performance multiple times in multiple ways brought to the surface the construction of an authoritative identity that students were undertaking. Other students, such as V whose script I quoted above, chose to include multiple roles in their podcasts. Because the first assignment required students to investigate the arguments made on multiple sides of an issue, role playing with more than one character allowed students to speak as authorities from different perspectives. For example, one pair of students produced a podcast about the issue of gun control: one of the students played the role of a newsperson who recounted the arguments by gun-control advocates, and the other student played the role of someone with an anti-gun-control perspective. By depicting a heated debate between the two, the authors were required to create an authoritative voice from two perspectives. When students construct multiple voices of authority, they learn not only can they perform an authoritative voice in an academic context but that any authoritative academic voice is part of a conversation and can be contended with; it is rhetorical.

Overview of the Context, the Assignment, and the Process

For writing students at the urban university where I teach, upper-division writing courses are challenging in my teaching experience. For example, in a 300-level, rhetoric-based advanced writing class I have taught for several semesters, medium-length research paper assignments often prompt reactions such as increased student silence in the class meetings following my initial discussion of the assignment or numerous questions from students in class and during my office hours about superficial mechanical features of the writing task rather than more substantial questions about invention and content. I guide students to use ancient rhetorical models to analyze current political debates and to construct their own writing about these debates. While my students nearly universally produce better papers in the end than they initially believe they are capable of, I am always in search of ways to make invention more useful and to help students approach their writing with more confidence rather than focusing prematurely on the daunting final research product. In an experiment toward this end, I used podcasting at the beginning of this course in two recent semesters. By prompting students to create their own podcasts at the beginning of the semester, the assignment helped mitigate much of the uneasiness with creating authority that in past semesters prevented students from producing useful early drafts of their research papers.

The assignment (see the Appendix) required students to work together in teams of two to produce a short, five-minute mp3 file[4] that would educate the class about a current controversial news issue they planned to write about over the course of the semester. The description stipulated that the podcast should take the format of a news presentation similar to a news broadcast we might hear on the radio. In order to help students assume the identity of a broadcast persona, students were prompted to begin the podcast with the phrase, "This just in . . ."

Students began by working with a partner to decide whose topics they would use for this activity. Then, they worked together to write a script for their podcast. The script was to be no more than two typed, double-spaced pages so that students did not exceed the five-minute time limit. They could break the script into two equal parts that each wrote separately, or they could write the script together. Some students chose to break the time up so that each produced a separate two-and-a-half-minute podcast on their own topic, but they worked as a team to share ideas and to help each other with the podcast recording process.

I advised students that the content of their podcasts should give the audience (the class and professor) an overview of the issue and encouraged them to include one or two particularly interesting examples or details. The assignment prompted them to think about how they would like to organize the script, as well as who would read it aloud for the podcast, an individual student or a combination of both partners. I encouraged them to be creative and have fun; while not required to include sound effects, some students chose to use editing programs such as Garage Band to weave sound bites and other effects into their performances.

As I explained in the assignment description, the main purpose of the assignment was for students to begin to clarify and narrow the topic of their first paper very early in the writing process. Because students continued with the same topic through two medium-length, scaffolded research papers in this course, narrowing their topics early was an important component of producing successful analytical writing. However, the process of narrowing the topic was a learning goal in itself and not merely a means to an end. Rather than an activity in isolation, the podcast performance was designed to help the class think communally about what kind of topic would work for a research paper and why. The brevity of the assignment encouraged students to narrow the topic to a manageable scope. Students were graded only on producing the podcast and not on whether they had a viable research topic, so the assignment was fairly low-stakes at 5% of the course grade. However, because the podcasts were played for the class, the element of conscious public performance inherent in the assignment encouraged students to take it seriously. The main motivation for completing the podcast was participating in the community of the class and getting feedback on the assignment.

In the full transcript of V's podcast below, you can see how he approached the assignment (V enlisted a friend from outside the class to play the role of "AJ the Host").

AJ: *Welcome everyone. This is AJ, your talk show host for tonight. The presidential debates are heating up, and free trade is one of the hottest topics right now. To discuss the issue, we have with us V, representative of investment corporations. Welcome to the show, Mr. V.*

V: *Thank you, AJ.*

AJ: *So, free trade has given corporations an unwarranted reason to outsource jobs in order to maximize their own profit, while our American workers are left unemployed. So why should we practice free trade?*

V: *Well, AJ, that's not exactly true. People say Americans are losing jobs. But the fact is that the unemployment rate has been stable. Outsourcing resulting from free trade means we have lower-cost imports and it's lowered costs for goods. And this is good for consumers, which means we have a higher standard of living, which is directly related to a growing economy and increasing per-capita GDP. Free trade works both ways, you see. Statistics show that we give up a few jobs, but in return are getting an increased number of jobs that are paying higher in our country. AJ, it's all about learning new skills and just joining the job market. Job retraining is the way to deal with it.*

AJ: *Uh, you said job retraining?*

V: *Yes!*

AJ: *Okay, then let's look at this clip from CNN about a certain Sona Shaw, whose brother, in fact, is unemployed.*

[AJ plays a clip of a woman explaining that she and her brother, both with degrees in engineering from excellent schools, are unemployed. She makes the argument that there is no lack of skills in the United States that would justify sending jobs overseas.]

AJ: *Well, geez, what are her choices now?*

V: *Uh, well, uh, uhhh. . .*

AJ: *Okay, well, let's move on. You also said free trade works both ways, but NAFTA's been in effect fourteen years and it's pretty obvious that it hasn't been benefitting us. Our half-a-trillion-dollar trade deficit is proof of that.* [Phone rings.]

AJ: *What, what is that?*

V: *Umm, sorry AJ, excuse me.*

AJ: *Are you serious, you, you're gonna answer that?*

V: *Yeah, it's very important, AJ. It's my boss.*

AJ: *We're on live right now!*

V: [answers phone] *Hello? Yeah, I'm on the show right now. What?! Are you serious? No, no you can't be serious. Hello? Hello?*

AJ: *What's wrong?*

V: *Um, I just got a call from my boss. He just told me that I got laid off. And a guy from India who will replace me will call to join the debate!*

AJ: *Oh, wow, uh, well I, uh, it's time for a short break, I guess. And I'll be back, if I still have my job.*

In this podcast, V has written a script in which he is an authority on the issue of free trade. He draws from his preliminary reading on issues of free trade and outsourcing of jobs and also on his personal experience in his workplace and with knowing people who have lost jobs due to outsourcing. He introduces the topic of free trade and has the host AJ ask questions about whether the United States should practice free trade. Through his character V, he represents the argument that free trade is creating more high-paying jobs in this country, while AJ implicitly argues that free trade is taking away jobs. Through this performative exchange, V embodies the research question of whether free trade is creating more or fewer jobs in the United States. Other sub-topics he mentions include NAFTA, the deficit, and the GDP.

After V played his podcast for the class, we discussed the research question that could emerge. We quickly realized that his topic is too broad for a medium-length research paper and that it would be helpful for him to narrow his question. We collectively brainstormed by asking V questions about what he had learned in his reading. In these conversations, V remained the expert, having read more than the rest of the class on his topic. He explained later that he initially understood his topic as free trade, but after our class discussion, he decided that his research question was more specific: whether the benefits of outsourcing jobs outweigh the costs. While he would need to modify his topic still a bit more as he learned more about the debate, he came away from the podcasting assignment with a specific research question that lead him to a focused research paper.

While this public vetting of research topics created communal goals early in the semester, it also gave students a chance to see each other's invention processes as they unfolded. No student struggled in isolation with a topic that didn't work. And while the process of narrowing the topic was indeed work, it was also fun for students/authorities and me the instructor/learner to engage in this communal goal. Perhaps more importantly, as students adopted an authoritative persona and maintained it through their post-podcast discussions and paper workshops, they began to see surface conventions of their papers (the elements students in past semesters had fixed on) as rhetorical choices associated with the persona they would develop in their academic writing.

Results

While I don't make absolute claims about the effects of student-generated podcasting, I have noticed some consistent changes in my advanced writing students' performances both in the classroom and in their writing. I think that these patterns indicate that it would be worthwhile for instructors to experiment with podcasting if they are noticing that their students have difficulty creating authority and engaging productively in their writing processes.

The assignment created a community in the classroom early on that evolved into productive workshop groups for the semester. Students became familiar and comfortable with each other early on, and this comfort manifested itself in more engaged writing groups in which students became invested in each other's progress and success over the course of the semester. (In fact, I often could not easily get students to stop workshopping at the end of class.) Perhaps most importantly, students sought feedback from each other rather than hesitantly sharing their writing because it was required. I saw students plan to e-mail each other outside of class to comment on additional drafts and sometimes form informal writing pairs. While students didn't maintain the same workshopping groups throughout the semester, they got used to presenting their work to one another and to thinking of the work of the class as communal.

The goal of listening to the podcasts in class was for students to help one another form viable research topics. To meet this goal, students needed to become invested in each other's success. The fact that they did invest in one another—that they collaborated—was, I believe, due to the performative nature of the assignment. Fishman et al. argue that because of the immediate nature of performance, it "encourages active participation and collaboration, and thus it models many of the qualities we value most in real-time new media writing" (226). I would add that it also mirrors some of the qualities that we generally value in writing: seeking feedback and considering one's audience as part of constructing one's authority and persona. As perspectives on performance studies from anthropology have highlighted, performance offers "alternative ways for imagining and enacting social relationships" (Fishman et al. 227). As students are reimagining their relationships to texts, they are also reimagining their relationships to the classroom. They came to see the workshop as a tool for constructing an identity in their writing rather than an exercise that they needed to complete.

Podcasting also enabled my students and me to see each assignment as part of a larger discursive project involving inquiry, discussion, research, drafting, and revising. It was a key part of scaffolding the major assignments for the course. The podcast assignment followed an annotated bibliography assignment and preceded the drafting of the first research paper. Students were first instructed to create an annotated bibliography of at least seven sources, covering a range of books, articles available through academic databases, and authoritative websites. I gave them the podcast assignment at the same time as the annotated bibliography assignment, explaining that the research they did for the annotated bibliography would be used later for the podcast assignment. In other words, producing a successful podcast depended upon producing a useful annotated bibliography because they needed the information gathered for the bibliography to write the script for the podcast.

The podcast assignment provided a rhetorical element to the annotated bibliography assignment that would not otherwise have existed. Students knew that the information they gathered for the annotated bibliography would later be presented to an audience of their peers as part of the script. They had to gain enough background on their potential paper topic to write a news story on the issue. They knew that the information had to be cohesive and tell a story about the issue—qualities that also help create an effective bibliography. Had the annotated bibliography not been linked to the performance of the podcast, students would have no impetus to imagine an audience broader than me, the grader. But because the drafting of the annotated bibliography overlapped with the podcasting process, the two assignments complemented each other by creating an investment in rhetorical awareness that students applied to both assignments. Students were able to imagine their peers as an audience more concretely than they might imagine the audience of the annotated bibliography if the end result was only a grade from me. The annotated bibliographies that they produced were markedly more cohesive, thorough, and useful than those produced by students in earlier semesters.

The podcast itself, of course, presented the clearest rhetorical situation. Because students knew that they would be presenting a recorded audio file to their peers, they had an immediate impetus to consider how best to communicate with that audience. As it turned out, they knew how to persuade each other better than I did. Students identified pathos, ethos, and logos during their invention processes without us yet having discussed these categories as part of an ancient concept of persuasion. They indirectly considered elements of classical invention that we would later learn directly, including definition, division, and comparison. They considered how to appeal to their audience, and decided how much to explain about the arguments they summarized. They arranged the information they gathered so that the shape of the debate was clear. With almost no exceptions, students wanted to have their podcasts well-received by their peers as indicated through their questions to me in class and over e-mail, through the time they invested in the assignment, and in their eagerness to hear class members' responses to their podcasts.

Surely, many factors were in play in addition to this assignment that led to my students' increased confidence during the semesters when I've used podcasting. I will need to research beyond three semesters in order to understand more specifically how podcasting worked synthetically with the other elements of the course. However, I do believe that podcasting has opened a window in my pedagogy by allowing student performance to be enacted through a digital audio medium.

Podcasting and Multimodal Discourse

Despite the primacy that composition classrooms typically give to writing while ignoring composing skills involved in multimodal communication, today's students are skilled at manipulating language in a wide range of media outside of the academy. This phenomenon has been recognized by Fishman et al. in their research through the Stanford Study of Writing, and by Cynthia L. Selfe in her research on multimodal composing. Also following this trend, a 2005 study by the Kaiser Family Foundation (KFF) described young people's lives as "media saturated." Studies such as the KFF's have been used to argue that incorporating technology more fully into teaching will provide a better real-world education for students (Jensen 19-20).

Yet, access to technology varies considerably from one academic institution to the next. At urban institutions with a non-traditional population, students have differential access to and experience with technology and media resources. While some professors move toward podcasting lectures on the premise that students are already familiar with mp3 files from experience at home and in social settings, this assumption does not hold universally. For example, a significant portion of my students were not familiar with mp3 files: while they may have listened to music in the form of an mp3 file, they were less inclined to know what an mp3 file was or to have recorded one themselves. Thus, an argument could be made that podcasting requires some students to learn new technology rather than capitalizing on technology they are already using outside the classroom. Additionally, any instructor using audio technology should be cognizant of the different learning styles and abilities. This assignment would not work the same way, for example, with deaf students. An instructor might consider an alternative (possibly a video with sign language) performative assignment during the invention process for students with alternative needs. Projects designed to incorporate technology into classes should be viewed, therefore, with an eye toward such issues of access and toward questions about the ultimate goal of using such technology.

At the same time as I point to these issues of access, I argue that multimodal composing can be a creative, effective part of the invention process for students at urban and traditional universities—and not only because it incorporates technology students are already using in their extracurricular lives (in fact, they may not be using the specific technologies that I am interested in experimenting with in my classes). Such technology is useful because it incorporates performance, a tangibly rhetorical approach to expression that can be useful during the invention process in writing. At its most effective, this performative epistemology enables students to embody an authority that transfers into their writing. The experience can lead writers to take more risks during the invention process and become more confident about their abilities to perform research and engage in the revision of their ideas. All of these benefits can ultimately make the writing process more successful for students.

Notes

1 In the first two years of the Stanford Study of Writing, Fishman et al. found that "nearly three quarters of the study's participants had had a high or very high degree of self-confidence in their writing abilities. However, [. . .] fewer than 10 percent of students maintained very high confidence in themselves as writers during that time" (231).

2 The association between positive experiences and the ability to take on writing tasks has also been discussed in self-efficacy research, though not specifically in terms of risk-taking. Self-efficacy, first studied by Albert Bandura, is the belief in one's ability to complete the tasks called for in order to achieve specific goals. Frank Pajares has applied Bandura's theory to academic writing contexts.
3 I have used a pseudonym for this student in this article. I have also obtained IRB approval for this study through Hunter College, CUNY's Institutional Review Board, and have followed informed consent protocol with all student participants.
4 In my assignment and in the article, I followed the popular convention of using the term "podcast" to refer to the mp3 audio files that my students recorded using a software program called Wimba Podcaster. While students in my course could download and play the mp3 files through an iPod or other mp3 player, we listened to the files through a computer in the classroom.

Works Cited

Bandura, Albert. *Self-Efficacy: The Exercise of Control*. New York: Worth, 1997. Print.

Bartholomae, David. "Inventing the University." *Cross-Talk in Comp Theory: A Reader*. Ed. Victor Villanueva, Jr. Urbana: NCTE, 1997. 623-54. Print.

Claycomb, Ryan. "Performing/Teaching/Writing: Performance Studies in the Composition Classroom." *Enculturation*. 6.1 (2008): n. pag. Web. 24 April 2009.

Fishman, Jenn, Andrea Lunsford, Beth McGregor, and Mark Otuteye. "Performing Writing, Performing Literacy." *CCC* 57.2 (2005): 224-252. Print.

Jensen, Amy Peterson. "Multimodal Literacy and Theatre Education." *Arts Education Policy Review* 109.5 (2008): 19-28. Print.

The Henry J. Kaiser Family Foundation. "Generation M: Media in the Lives of 8-18 Year Olds." Kaiser Family Foundation. 9 March 2005. Web. 24 April 2009.

Kopelson, Karen. "Dis/Integrating the Gay/Queer Binary: 'Reconstructed Identity Politics' for a Performative Pedagogy." *College English* 65.1 (2002): 17-35. Print.

Lindemann, Erika. *A Rhetoric for Writing Teachers*. 4th ed. New York: Oxford UP, 2001. Print.

Love, Meredith. "Composing Through the Performative Screen: Translating Performance Studies into Writing Pedagogy." *Composition Studies* 35.2 (2007): 11-30. Print.

McLaren, Peter. *Schooling as Ritual Performance: Towards a Political Economy of Educational Symbols and Gestures*. 2nd ed. London: Routledge, 1993. Print.

Pajares, Frank, and Margaret J. Johnson. "Confidence and Competence in Writing: The Role of Self-Efficacy, Outcome Expectancy, and Apprehension." *Research in the Teaching of English* 28.3 (1994): 313-331. Print.

Schechner, Richard. "What is Performance Studies Anyway?" *The Ends of Performance*. Ed. Peggy Phelan and Jill Lane. New York: New York UP, 1998. 357-62. Print.

Selfe, Cynthia L. "The Movement of Air, the Breath of Meaning: Aurality and Multimodal Composing." *CCC* 60.4 (2009): 616-663. Print.

Tremel, Justin, and Jamie Jesson. "Podcasting in the Rhetoric Classroom." *Currents in Electronic Literacy* 10 (2007): n. pag. Web. 24 April 2009.

Appendix: Assignment

Podcasting Assignment: "This just in. . ."

Purpose: The purpose of this assignment is for you to work on clarifying and narrowing the topic of your first paper. Narrowing your topic early will help you produce a successful analysis paper in the end. Through this activity, you will work with your classmates to clarify your topic and to get feedback on ways to narrow the topic further, if necessary.

Assignment: Your assignment is to work together in teams of two to produce a short (less than 5-minute) audio podcast (mp3 file) that educates the class about the issue you will write about for your first paper. The podcast should take the format of a news presentation similar to a news broadcast you might hear on the radio, and should begin with the phrase, "This just in. . ."

Begin by working with your partner to choose a topic. While you and your partner may write about separate topics, decide as a team which of your topics you will use for this activity. Then, work together to write a script for your podcast. Your script should be no more than two typed, double-spaced pages so that you don't exceed the five-minute time limit. You can break the script into two equal parts that you each write separately, or you can both write the script together.

Your purpose is to give your audience (the class and your professor) an overview of the issue; you may wish to include one or two particularly interesting examples or details about the issue. Think about how you would like to organize the script, as well as who will read the script (you, your partner, or a combination). You may also choose to include sound effects. Be creative and have fun!

You will play your finished podcast for the class. After we hear each podcast, the class will discuss it and make suggestions for narrowing the topic, if necessary.

Schedule: Presentation in library—week 2
Presentation on podcasting—week 2
Script-writing time in class—week 2
Scripts due (I'll look over them)—week 3
Podcasting takes place—week 3
We listen to podcasts—week 4

Grade: This assignment is worth 5 points of your informal assignment grade.

TCU

Learning to change the world™

Offering M.A. and Ph.D. programs in English, as well as a new Ph.D. program in Rhetoric and Composition, TCU provides students with a tradition of excellence in graduate studies that combines intellectual development with practical training and professional mentoring.

Qualities that draw students to our department:

◊   A nationally respected faculty

◊   Competitive, multi-year fellowships and a 1-1 teaching load for Graduate Instructors

◊   Opportunities for experience working for the New Media Writing Studio

◊   An outstanding record of student placement and publication

To learn more about the programs in rhetoric, composition, and literature at TCU, visit us at

www.eng.tcu.edu

Not Just One Shot: Extending the Dialogue about Information Literacy in Composition Classes

Margaret Artman, Erica Frisicaro-Pawlowski, and Robert Monge

While composition programs are frequently responsible for teaching basic research writing, it is still common practice to limit lessons in information literacy to "one-shot" library instruction sessions. This practice reinforces the perception that the research process is separate from (and simpler than) the writing process, that teaching students effective research practices can be reduced to a single, skills-based class session, and that, ultimately, literacy in information is only useful if tied to the academic research paper. We argue that writing and information literacy are complimentary processes that need to be integrated into multiple, contextual classroom sessions. Through collaboration and shared responsibility, writing teachers and librarians can better incorporate information literacy instruction within composition programs and improve students' research options and behaviors.

Introduction

Instructors across the disciplines would probably agree that students' ability to incorporate research within their writing is an essential facet of college education. Yet, most compositionists would assert that simply helping students use and cite research in their writing is not sufficient to make them more thoughtful writers or more successful students. Instead, writing instructors have increasingly come to see information literacy (IL) as a key element in a range of critical activities. According to Diane VanderPol, Jeanne M. Brown, and Patricia Iannuzzi, information literacy enables students "to determine the nature of information needed to solve a problem, find targeted information and evaluate its reliability and usefulness, apply and analyze the information to create new knowledge, and function with an understanding of the ethical and financial contexts of their information use" (12). Twenty-first century teachers of writing recognize that because our students have an excess of information resources at their disposal, creating rich opportunities for undergraduate engagement in diverse, dynamic research projects that develop such literacies is absolutely essential.

Despite the proliferation of information resources, however, a recent Project Information Literacy report notes that students' habits as information seekers appear slow to change. According to the report's authors: "students exhibited little inclination to vary the frequency or order of their use [of information resources], regardless of their information goals and despite the plethora of other online and in person information resources—including librarians—that were available to them" (Head and Eisenberg 3). As such, we can conclude that many students will attempt to complete all of their college writing assignments using only a handful of the resources at their disposal.

Because composition instructors commonly bear responsibility for general research instruction, helping students to take advantage of such resources—and to use them creatively, purposefully, and thoughtfully— should be a prominent goal in our pedagogy and curriculum design. Indeed, in highlighting the importance of information literacy in all disciplines and at every academic level, professional organizations such as the American Library Association (ALA) and the Association of College and Research Libraries (ACRL) have effectively set the stage for those who wish to infuse both writing and research across the curriculum (see also D'Angelo and Maid; Grafstein; Mackey and Jacobson; Information Literacy Articulation Group). Yet even as institutions are beginning to embrace direct information literacy instruction as part of the twenty-first century college curriculum, sustained attention to students' use of information resources has not yet become a central curricular component of first-year composition, where information and research instruction is too often relegated to a one-shot library session. Librarians use the term "one-shot instruction" to describe brief (50-75 minute) library sessions in which they are asked to teach students all the skills they need to become information literate (Reitz 499). The term is thus meant to both describe and convey the futility of these sessions. Instead of providing any meaningful sense of what it means to engage the complexity of scholarly research, one-shot instructions provide just enough basic skill training for the student to find the 3-5 sources required to write their composition paper. Even though this approach has obvious shortcomings, in our own experiences at ten colleges and universities, one-shot instruction was the primary means of introducing students to research in first-year writing course work. Such trends, while anecdotal, seem to indicate that IL has not yet been adequately and practically integrated within introductory composition classrooms or curricula. This article will consider why and how writing instructors should engage in the conversation about information literacy on a professional level, as well as how instructors and librarians can collaborate to address this knowledge gap in student writing.

Research, Writing, Reciprocity: Resisting the Skills Mindset

Over the past decade, composition specialists have begun to address the importance of pairing effective information literacy instruction with instruction in composition. In reviewing publications on information literacy and composition, however, two prevailing patterns emerge. First, prior to 2009, the majority of scholarship that seeks to theorize the influence of IL instruction within composition classrooms—or the role of writing in information literacy instruction—appears in journals outside the field of Composition. While two recent articles on composition and information literacy have appeared in journals such as *Composition Forum* and *WPA: Writing Program Administration*,[1] articles on integrating information literacy and the writing curriculum published earlier in the decade by Rolf Norgaard and Barbara D'Angelo and Barry Maid appeared in journals devoted to library and information science. Second, and perhaps more significant, scholarship on the integration of information literacy and writing instruction produced to date is overwhelmingly local. Published accounts on collaborative IL instruction commonly represent how particular programs have integrated library and research instruction within specific writing courses, or using particular collaborative models. Even though awareness of the role information literacy plays in developing effective writing strategies appears to be growing, we agree with Norgaard that "given how much classroom practice in rhetoric and composition involves helping students with inquiry and research, it is nothing short of surprising how little the field has written about information literacy and library collaboration, especially if one is looking for more than anecdotal reports of local practice" ("Contributions" 125). For nearly a decade, calls to reflect upon collective institutional practices and to build mutually supportive, engaged, and collaborative theories of blended IL and writing instruction have instead resulted in a fragmented and tenuous disciplinary perspective on the role of IL in writing instruction.

This tendency to resist a more comprehensive disciplinary understanding of the global, recursive relationships between information literacy and student writing may serve to perpetuate outmoded notions of what it means to be information literate, or what it means to compose in a digital age. As with writing, practice in research and information literacy has evolved from a concept largely associated with a set of discrete skills required to produce a polished and complete product (e.g., locating, gathering, and documenting sources), into a reciprocal and sophisticated process for interpreting, integrating, and sharing information. Norgaard, in the first of his guest columns published in *Reference and Information Services Quarterly*, highlights parallels between the development of information literacy and that of composition by outlining central misperceptions influencing work in both fields, most significantly:

> that information literacy is a neutral, technological skill that is, at heart, merely functional or performative. Rhetoric and composition has a long history of confronting similar misperceptions about reading and writing. Complaints that Johnny can't read, or that Jane can't write, easily promote

the notion that literacy is a neutral, discrete, context-free skill. These perceptions also remain in play regarding information literacy. ("Contributions" 125)

Just as compositionists have responded to such misperceptions with more nuanced, more complex models of writing, so have librarians worked to craft more sophisticated—and realistic—notions of what it means to discover, process, develop, and meaningfully utilize information for exploratory and communicative purposes.[2]

Despite progress in reconceptualizing both information literacy and composition as rich, productive, and complex processes, James Elmborg argues that theoretical and programmatic divisions have thwarted attempts to build from common notions of literacy valued by both compositionists and librarians. In his work, "Libraries and Writing Centers in Collaboration: A Basis in Theory," Elmborg notes:

> The recursiveness of the research/writing process is related at least in part to the recurring interplay between writing and information. By segregating the research process from the writing process, we have obscured the fact and thereby impoverished both the writing process and the research process. This segregation reflects institutional divisions, but not the reality of student work. (11)

Unfortunately, all too often, composition professionals have played a role in perpetuating such divisions. Though our programs frequently bear the responsibility for teaching basic research writing to first-year students, it is still common practice to either disregard the expertise our librarian colleagues may lend to IL instruction, or, conversely, to "farm out" lessons in information literacy to one-shot library instruction sessions.[3] These practices can, in turn, serve to reinforce the perception that the research process is separate from (and more facile than) the writing process, that teaching students effective research practices can be reduced to a single, skills-based class session, and that, ultimately, literacy in information is only useful or valuable if tied to that well-worn (and ill-formed) genre, the academic research paper. In this sense, one-shot instruction mirrors misperceptions regarding literacy education that compositionists have sought to change. According to Chris Fosen, "under the skills mindset, individual composition classes reproduce education as the acquisition of basic tools that have value only in the progress toward a degree, not in their meaningful or disciplinary use" (20). By teaching research as a single and discrete unit disconnected from rhetorical concerns, we powerfully influence the ways students come to understand and engage information. According to Alison J. Head and Michael B. Eisenberg, the skills mindset continues to shape students' perceptions of research, as "findings suggest students conceptualize research, especially tasks associated with seeking information, as a competency learned by rote, rather than as an opportunity to learn, develop, or expand upon an information-gathering strategy which leverages the wide range of resources available to them" (1).

Just as theories of process served to revolutionize the teaching and administration of writing courses in the last decades of the twentieth century, reconceptualizing the teaching and placement of information literacy in our writing programs is crucial in these early years of the twenty-first century. In particular, developing programs that recognize the complexity, the difficulty, and the centrality of information literacy within contemporary writing environments may prove essential to counteracting the skills mindset, in that research requires responsible, inquiry-driven consideration of "meaningful" uses of information. As noted by Norgaard, "thinking of information literacy as 'shaped' by writing—writing theory, writing instruction, and the very writing process itself" enriches composition as both a practice and a field ("Contributions" 125). Yet, in order to teach students to make "meaningful or disciplinary use" of information as both tool and concept (Fosen 20), our programs must embrace the technical and disciplinary knowledge of research and teaching librarians.

The work begun by research and teaching librarians clearly provides fertile ground for collaborative, informed, and creative approaches to sharing responsibility for instruction in writing and research. In their work "A Blended Method for Integrating Information Literacy Instruction into English Composition Classes," librarians Leslie Sult and Vicki Mills indicate that practically and philosophically, there is a "natural fit and shared goals of information literacy and English composition programs," as both "writing and researching are viewed as non-linear processes and both require individuals to work back and forth through a number of stages of discovery, development, and critical thinking" (369-70). To prove their point, Sult and Mills provide a table drawing clear parallels between the Council of Writing Program Administrators' Outcomes Statement and the ACRL Standards for Information Literacy. Indeed, the ACRL indicates that successful information literacy programs "depend on collaboration between classroom faculty, academic administrators, librarians and other information professionals" ("Information Literacy for Faculty and Administrators"). As Sult and Mills explain, "For a multitude of reasons, budgetary constraints, personnel reductions, and questions of efficacy, libraries and librarians are being challenged to develop more integrated methods for assisting faculty, instructors, and students in teaching and learning information literacy skills" (368). To do so, university libraries often reach out to established programs such as first-year experience seminars, first-year writing courses, writing centers, service learning courses, or writing-intensive courses. All of these partnerships can be successful; yet, "[t]hroughout the library instruction literature, it has long been held that targeting first year English composition courses is an efficient and effective means of incorporating information literacy into the curriculum" because it is typically required for new students and requires research-based writing (369).

Composition specialists can bring a wealth of experience and knowledge regarding student writing practices to bear in such partnerships. However, we must also remain mindful of *how* we might successfully incorporate information literacy within first-year writing programs. According to Randall McClure and Kellian Clink, information literacy problems could be caused by "too many people working in isolation" (131) and perhaps no other symptom of this problem is as pronounced as one-shot instruction—an inefficient and inadequate means of preparing students to incorporate meaningful research into their writing. Yet, one-shot instruction persists in many first-year writing programs despite the focus on writing and research as complimentary processes and the knowledge that, for library instruction to be effective, it has to occur in several sessions throughout a term and within multiple contexts. According to David A. Sousa, practice "refers to learners repeating a skill over time. It begins with the rehearsal of the new learning in working memory. Later, the memory is recalled from long-term storage and additional rehearsal follows. The quality of the rehearsals and the learner's knowledge base will largely determine the outcome of each practice" (97). Repetition cannot occur in a one-shot instruction because of the severe time limitation. Also, there is no way to ensure students will perform quality repetition outside of the session. After a demonstration or explanation of a few research options, the student is left with only a few minutes of practice for something they are likely to forget once they have their needed sources. Studies such as Project Information Literacy indicate that students are fairly rigid in their research process, unwilling or unable to expand their research agendas and procedures (Head and Eisenberg 14-15); one-shot instruction thus cannot provide the support, motivation, or attention required to change information literacy behaviors.

The time limitations in one-shot instruction sessions also fail to provide an adequate means of presenting the information in different contexts. This is essential for encoding (a process that relates new information to information already in long-term memory thus making it easier to recall when needed): "Retrieval, then, is very much influenced by the context of encoding. This suggests for instruction that many different contexts or examples may be important to discuss during the presentation of new concepts. In this way, students will have many cues available to assist in encoding that may later be used for recall" (Driscoll 101). One-shot instructions simply do not allow for the multiple presentations of contexts that would allow for long-term memory retrieval.

Additionally, time limitations imposed by one-shot instruction may inhibit or obscure essential connections between research contexts and writing processes. According to the Project Information Literacy report, students' efforts in establishing a context for their research are "key to understanding how students operationalize and prioritize their course-related and everyday life research activities" (Head and Eisenberg 7). Based on their preliminary findings, Head and Eisenberg define four research contexts students must engage in fulfilling both academic and everyday tasks:

1. Big picture: Finding out background for defining and selecting a topic
2. Language: Figuring out what words and terms associated with a topic may mean
3. Situational: Gauging how far to go with research, based on surrounding circumstances
4. Information-gathering: finding, accessing, and securing relevant research resources. (7)

Clear links exist between this contextual model and rhetorical models, both classic and contemporary: specifically, between *situational research* and analysis of a rhetorical situation; between both *language research* and *information-gathering* and elements of genre or discourse analysis; and between *big-picture research* and elements of invention, definition, and exposition. One-shot instruction by necessity isolates procedural *information-seeking* behaviors from the more complex range of behaviors that allow students to make informed choices regarding potential uses of information in particular rhetorical contexts. Yet, it also appears to serve as an all-too-common means through which first-year writing programs attempt to address the pivotal role research can play in the writing process.[4]

Collectively, we can do much better—particularly if we heed the advice of McClure and Clink and work collaboratively, rather than in isolation. Instead of one-shot sessions, librarians could seek to create alliances with faculty in order to improve students' research options and behaviors. Specifically, librarians hope to provide information literacy instruction and support at multiple points during a project or a term, providing repeated opportunities in which students can practice a range of approaches to research. Fortunately, writing instructors appear increasingly interested in creating partnerships that facilitate library instruction in order to improve students' use of information in written research.

To date, attempts to measure the success of such partnerships have focused on the written products students submit after taking part in a collaborative information literacy initiative. For example, in "Collaboration is Key: Librarians and Composition Instructors Analyze Student Research and Writing," Barratt et al. study research practices of students enrolled in the University of Georgia's first-year composition program, asking whether a combination of library instruction and clear assignment guidelines improves students' research citations. In their examination of 5,246 citations culled from student writing across 40 FYC sections, students relied on Web sites 51 percent of the time (42). Half of the sections participated in library instruction sessions [LI] and half of the sections had no library instruction [NLI] (46). The total number of citations per assignment was nearly the same per assignment [LI: 65 citations, NLI: 66 citations] (47). In addition, the number of times students used Web sites were the same [LI: 50 percent, NLI: 51 percent] (47). The only "noticeable effect of library instruction lay in the number of books and articles the students cited" (47). NLI classes used more books [24 percent versus 17 percent] and LI used more articles [29 percent versus 21 percent] (47).

To understand how the assignment and library instruction influence citations, the researchers then analyzed one assignment in four classes, examining "citations within the context of individual writers, teachers, assignments, and library instruction" (37) and considering each of the following factors: the type of information resource (book, journal, Web site, etc.); how citations are used within the student essays (advance an argument, make a point, meet an assignment requirement); and how the teachers' written assignment instructions influence citation quality (report information, choose one side of an issue, convince an audience) (49-54). Based on their findings, they conclude:

> Library instruction and carefully considered teacher assignments—in particular, written instructions—*do* have a positive influence on the quality of the research that students perform for their first-year composition courses. As predicted by previous studies, neither factor alone prompts the best research method; written exhortations and library instruction must work in tandem. Librarians and instructors need to focus as much on crafting an effective assignment together as they do on teaching students information literacy and composition skills. (54)

If we understand information literacy as a mix of choosing the appropriate sources and using the sources appropriately, librarians and instructors can work together to identify teaching strategies that not only assist students in finding information but also in using that information purposefully. Further, this collaboration must not be reserved until students are in the process of conducting or beginning their research, but must be part of instructional planning envisioned by the instructor or writing program administrator. If this sort of cooperation appears to improve student writing (in terms of the final products produced through such partnerships), then our efforts as compositionists and WPAs must focus on the collaborative processes that facilitate productive interaction between library and writing instructors.

Incorporating IL in the Writing Curriculum: The View from the Library

While a growing body of research is working to assess the effectiveness of library partnerships within particular programs (see, for example, Brady et.al.; Holliday and Fagerheim; Sult and Mills) or to achieve particular ends (Macklin; Mackey and Jacobson), librarians have been developing various alternatives to one-shot instruction. In "Information Literacy and Higher Education: Placing the Academic Library in the Center of a Comprehensive Solution," Edward K. Owusu-Ansah argues for three types of library instruction: "Course-related and course-integrated instruction, the two most popular methods for bibliographic instruction, and independent credit courses remain the most viable vehicles for delivering information literacy instruction" (11). Similarly, McClure and Clink indicate that problems in effectively integrating information literacy instruction in English composition courses "are best solved through innovative collaborations between the information experts (librarians) and writing experts (EC teachers). These partnerships might involve interactive Web-based supplements, co-requisite information literacy courses, and co-taught writing courses" (131).

Librarians have, for some time, lent their expertise to composition students in the form of course-related instruction. Course-related instruction refers to library instruction that, in addition to a one-shot library instruction or workshop, provides additional resources related to the course. The librarian works with the instructor to develop these resources, though contact with the students is typically limited to the one-shot session. More effective strategies, in terms of establishing meaningful collaborative efforts between writing instructors and librarians, involve the creation of additional resources such as subject or class guides related to the course. These Web-based guides provide a list of resources with a short description and Web link. They can include a list of library databases, Web sites, and other relevant information. Additional Web-based instruction can be provided on how to use these resources (for example, a video on searching JSTOR or a tutorial on scholarly versus peer-reviewed sources). These additional resources are housed on the library home page or in a course management system.

The advantage of course-related instruction is that it can provide additional demonstration and instruction opportunities through Web-based tutorials as well as providing a richer source of assignment-related resources for the student to explore. Further, such resources can be made available to all stakeholders involved in information literacy education—librarians, teachers, and students—thereby creating an integrated network of materials capable of extending instruction beyond the limitations of a single class or course. The disadvantage is that there is no way to ensure the quality of skill repetition or opportunities for encoding, as students may simply ignore these additional resources and tutorials.

Another alternative involves course-integrated library instruction: "a research and/or library component built into an academic course description as an essential part of the course" (LaGuardia et al. 55). In the course-integrated instruction model, the librarian has a presence in the course from the beginning of the term. This is accomplished with contact information in both the syllabus and course management system and with a live or face-to-face introduction on the first day of class. The librarian works with the faculty member to design specific library assignments related to the course (e.g., advanced Internet research, finding articles in library databases, or using podcasts for research). A brief in-class demo or library session is given prior to each assignment. These instructions can also take the form of self-paced, Web-based units. These assignments/Web-based units will be delivered during the term in short segments with relevant discussions related to each instruction. The assignments/Web-based units themselves may or may not have any impact on the final grade.

The advantage of course-integrated instruction is that it facilitates a higher quality of practice as the librarian can work with students one-on-one to improve their research skills. The breakdown of library instruction into smaller components allows multiple contexts for information to be presented, creating a greater opportunity for encoding and further attention to the importance of using research sources purposefully or strategically. Also, course-integrated instruction encourages communication and multiple points of contact between the students and librarian, and it may also help to address a key issue highlighted in the Project Information Literacy report: namely, students primarily turn to their instructors for guidance on research, rather than to librarians who specialize in research instruction. According to the report, "eight out of 10 of the respondents reported rarely, if ever, turning to librarians for help with course-related research assignments" (Head and Eisenberg 3). Preliminary research on course-integrated instruction indicates that more extensive exposure to research librarians can reverse this pattern. For example, in "Taking Library Instruction into the Online Classroom," Amy C. York and Jason M. Vance conducted a survey of librarians embedded in course management systems: "According to 70% of respondents, students 'often' or 'always' contact the embedded librarian (63% and 7%, respectively), and only 30% reported that students 'seldom' contact them" (206).

By working together to design assignments, as Randall McClure claims, "librarian-teacher partners will certainly learn more about their shared writing and researching goals, thus likely to improve both library and writing instruction in the process" (71). Further, from a programmatic perspective, course-integrated instruction can offer opportunities for WPAs to encourage professional development among teaching staff, to assess the effectiveness of information literacy initiatives, and to glean feedback from both instructional and library staff regarding students' writing and research practices. The disadvantage of course-integrated instruction is that while the depth of the library assignments/Web-based units is considerably greater than a one-shot instruction, it is unusual for significant portions of the course to contain information literacy instruction. Also, if no credit or grade is attached to completing the assignments/Web-based units, students may not be motivated to engage in this type of instruction.

Credit-bearing instruction "requires approval within the curriculum to carry institutional credit. These classes meet repeatedly and regularly and are library counterparts to academic courses" (LaGuardia et al. 56). *Credit* is the term that stands out in this type of library instruction. It requires a more substantial amount of information literacy instruction, and it has the consequences of a grade. Unfortunately, libraries that pursue credit-bearing information literacy instruction have advocated for an independent course. In addition to being difficult to add to the curriculum and nearly impossible to mandate as a requirement for graduation, these independent information literacy courses have been critiqued because they only teach information literacy separated from a real world context. According to Ann Grafstein,

> there is a risk in carrying too far the dichotomy between information seeking as a process and more concrete subject-based knowledge. The risk is that of isolating entirely information-seeking skills from knowledge, thereby losing sight of information-seeking skills as a tool whose ultimate goal is the synthesis of information into knowledge. (200)

While it makes sense to argue for additional information literacy instruction in upper-division, discipline-based courses, there is also a need to add a credit of information literacy instruction to existing composition courses. Boise State University, University of Utah, Daniel Webster College, and West Virginia University are examples of writing programs taking this approach (Estrem; Holliday and Fagerheim; Hearn; Brady et al.). Composition courses already have a place in the curriculum, are required for graduation, and can be a place to teach information-seeking skills in combination with the synthesis of knowledge. However, a composition course should not give up a credit of instruction to accommodate information literacy. Instead, a credit hour of information literacy could be added to a composition course in order to ensure a more integrated approach to instruction. For example, in "Integrating Information Literacy with a Sequenced English Composition Curriculum," Wendy Holliday and Britt Fagerheim describe how a writing-information literacy course would work: "The curriculum is divided into four lessons. Two lessons take place in the English classroom and last for 30-35 minutes, and two take place in the library and last for approximately 50 minutes" (179). Alternate models for integrated credit-bearing information literacy instruction include a hybrid of classroom instruction and Web-based units that are completed entirely online.

Ultimately, librarians can collaborate with faculty to design specific information literacy outcomes and objectives that fit particular course structures or program designs. Such collaboration is appropriate and useful in upper-division research or *capstone* courses (for example, discipline-specific research methods courses or courses that support senior research projects); yet, it can also enhance IL instruction in first-year course work. When designing collaborative arrangements in first-year programs, McClure argues "WPAs should take the leadership role in forming these partnerships, since they are the ones in charge of courses that nearly all undergraduates take" (71). Specifically, McClure recommends using WPA and ACRL resources "in local conversations among compositionists and librarians to determine what values, outcomes and standards for researching and writing they share" (71). Given the array of possibilities made possible by developments in library instruction, such conversations are surely crucial. However, it is also clear that integrating IL instruction within composition course work involves more than just *managing* options for teaching writing and information literacy as complementary, integrated activities. According to McClure, influencing "information behaviors" involves resourceful collaboration, requiring composition specialists to partner with information specialists in order to facilitate initiatives, pedagogies, and linkages that extend beyond disciplinary, physical, and institutional boundaries (71-2). For example, at one of our institutions, the WPA's office was recently relocated to a library and information commons and this physical location facilitates collaboration among writing, library, and academic support staff. The WPA's proximity to research librarians, as well as to the learning center and academic advising offices housed in the commons, has led to greater coordination of support services for first-year students, as well as the incorporation of IL as a more distinct component of the first-year writing curriculum. In another example, two of the authors attended Information Literacy Summits with college librarians and instructors across the state to discuss, create, and revise the Information Literacy Proficiencies (see Appendix), which would be enacted across their state university system. In addition, they meet weekly to make IL a clear part of composition and plan ways to involve more instructors in face-to-face and Web-based IL instruction. Currently, they are conducting a pilot study of course-integrated library instruction with a librarian and composition instructor team-taught course.

Conclusion

While the participation of individual composition instructors is important to this type of collaboration, D'Angelo and Maid suggest, "A great deal of time and energy are spent on advocacy and frequently individual efforts are not sustainable beyond the work of individual librarians or librarian-faculty team" (213). In particular, WPAs are in a unique position to encourage program-wide collaboration because of their administrative status (McClure 71). Since many college librarians are not considered faculty, they often have limited influence over institutional and curricular policies. Working collaboratively with WPAs can thus improve the likelihood of reform in the delivery of research and information instruction. Further, because WPAs are commonly responsible not only for first-year writing curricula, but also for facilitating faculty development within WAC and WID programs, their collaborative work with librarians has the potential to influence instruction after the first year. By helping faculty from across the disciplines incorporate meaningful IL assignments and instruction in their courses, WPAs and their collaborative library partners can encourage the development of additional context-specific approaches to research writing beyond the composition program. Such efforts are integral to supporting students' research and sustaining their development as writers throughout their academic careers.

Without a doubt, establishing more effective information literacy instruction within writing courses requires reflective, equitable, ethical, and ongoing participation among all faculty. Is this extra effort worth it? On a personal level, it could be if, as Elmborg suggests, the timing, personalities, and institutional context align (1). According to one audience member in attendance when we presented parts of this article at the 2009 WPA conference, she was happy to have someone else share the work. Yet, that may not be enough. On a larger scale, this type of collaboration, as many studies attest, improves student research performance because it introduces "students to academic writing as a complex, recursive learning process based on broad and open-minded information seeking" (Deitering and Jameson 78). Research skills cannot be taught in "one shot," just as writing cannot be taught in one term.

Notes

1 Brady et al. explain how they incorporate IL at West Virginia University. McClure analyzes student use of advocacy and commercial Web sites in their research papers. In his conclusion, he makes a call for WPAs to "take a leadership role" in forming partnerships with academic and research librarians (71).

2 For more extensive discussions of IL definitions and review of the literature, see ACRL "Information Literacy Competency Standards"; Brady et al; Eisenberg; and Rockman and Associates. For an overview of sample IL Proficiencies, see Appendix.

3 There is no current research about how composition instructors' knowledge of IL influences what they teach to students. Anecdotal evidence suggests that, much like their students, writing faculty tend to teach the few databases and skills with which they are familiar. This problem may even be exacerbated

when graduate students or instructors with limited experience teach composition classes. In other words, students who receive research instruction only from composition faculty may be learning a limited number of options available to them and only from the viewpoint of the particular writing instructor's own research background. This is why partnering with librarians is so important—it is not uncommon for librarians to hear comments from instructors such as "I learn something new every time I bring in a class" after a library instruction.

4 The emphasis on information-gathering skills within one-shot IL instruction sessions may also inadvertently undermine students' inherent motivation for pursuing independent research. According to the 2009 Project Information Literacy report, students' "need for big-picture context, or background about a topic, was the trigger for beginning course-related (65%) or everyday life research (63%)" (Head and Eisenberg 3). By deemphasizing elements of the research process related to invention and definition, in particular, one-shot instruction may thus impede processes of exploration important to student engagement in writing projects.

Works Cited

Association of College and Research Libraries (ACRL). "Information Literacy Competency Standards for Higher Education." *American Library Association*, 2000. Web. 10 Oct. 2009.

———. "Information Literacy for Faculty and Administrators." *American Library Association*, 2009. Web. 10 Oct. 2009.

Barratt, Caroline Carson, Kristin Nielsen, Christy Desmet, and Ron Balthazor. "Collaboration is Key: Librarians and Composition Instructors Analyze Student Research and Writing." *Portal: Libraries and the Academy* 9.1 (2009): 37-56. Print.

Brady, Laura, Nathalie Singh-Corcoran, Jo Ann Dadisman, and Kelly Diamond. "A Collaborative Approach to Information Literacy: First-Year Composition, Writing Center, and Library Partnerships at West Virginia University." *Composition Forum* 19 (Spring 2009): n. pag. Web. 30 Sept. 2009.

D'Angelo, Barbara J., and Barry M. Maid. "Moving Beyond Definitions: Implementing Information Literacy Across the Curriculum." *The Journal of Academic Librarianship* 30.3 (2004): 212-217. Print.

Deitering, Anne-Marie, and Sara Jameson. "Step by Step through the Scholarly Conversation: A Collaborative Library/Writing Faculty Project to Embed Information Literacy and Promote Critical Thinking in First Year Composition at Oregon State University." *College & Undergraduate Libraries* 15.1-2 (2008): 57-79. Print.

Driscoll, Marcy P. *Psychology of Learning for Instruction*. 3rd ed. Boston: Pearson, 2005. Print.

Eisenberg, Michael B. "Information Literacy: Essential Skills for the Information Age." *DESIDOC Journal of Library & Information Technology* 28.2 (March 2008): 39-47. Print.

Elmborg, James K. "Libraries and Writing Centers in Collaboration: A Basis in Theory." *Centers for Learning: Writing Centers and Libraries in Collaboration*.

Ed. James K. Elmborg and Sheril Hook. Chicago: Association of College and Research Libraries, 2005. Print. Publications in Librarianship No. 58.

Estrem, Heidi. "Research Program Administrators: Convergences and Collisions Among Writing Programs and Libraries." *Council of Writing Program Administrators Conference*. Radisson University Hotel, U of Minnesota-Twin Cities, Minneapolis. 18 July 2009. Roundtable presentation.

Fosen, Chris. "'University Courses, Not Department Courses': Composition and General Education." *Composition Studies* 34.1 (2006): 11-33. Print.

Frisicaro-Pawlowski, Erica, Margaret Artman, and Robert Monge. "Mis/Understanding Information Literacy: WPAs, Librarians, and the General Education Curriculum." *Council of Writing Program Administrators Conference*. Radisson University Hotel, U of Minnesota-Twin Cities, Minneapolis. 17 July 2009. Panel presentation.

Grafstein, Ann. "A Discipline-Based Approach to Information Literacy." *Journal of Academic Librarianship* 28.4 (2002): 197-204. Print.

Head, Alison J., and Michael B. Eisenberg. "Lessons Learned: How College Students Seek Information in the Digital Age." *Project Information Literacy Progress Report*. U of Washington's Information School, 1 Dec. 2009. Web. 7 Dec. 2009.

Hearn, Michael R. "Embedding a Librarian in the Classroom: An Intensive Information Literacy Model." *Reference Services Review* 33.2 (2005): 219-227. Print.

Holliday, Wendy, and Britt Fagerheim. "Integrating Information Literacy with a Sequenced English Composition Curriculum." *Portal: Libraries and the Academy* 6.2 (2006): 169-184. Print.

Information Literacy Articulation Group of Greater Portland. "Information Literacy Proficiencies for Students Ready to Move Into Upper-division Coursework." 10 April 2008. Web. 15 July 2009.

LaGuardia, Cheryl, Michael Blake, Lawrence Dowler, Laura Farwell, Caroline M. Kent, and Ed Tallent. *Teaching the New Library: A How-To-Do-It Manual for Planning and Designing Instructional Programs*. New York: Neal-Schuman, 1996. Print.

Mackey, Thomas P., and Trudy E. Jacobson. "Integrating Information Literacy in Lower- and Upper-Level Courses: Developing Scalable Models for Higher Education." *JGE: The Journal of General Education* 53.3-4 (2004): 201-224. Print.

Macklin, Alexius Smith. "Integrating Information Literacy Using Problem-Based Learning." *Reference Services Review* 29.4 (2001): 306-313. Print.

McClure, Randall. "Examining the Presence of Advocacy and Commercial Websites in Research Essays of First-Year Composition Students." *WPA: Writing Program Administration* 32.3 (Spring 2009): 49-74. Print.

McClure, Randall, and Kellian Clink. "How Do You Know That? An Investigation of Student Research Practices in the Digital Age." *Portal: Libraries and the Academy* 9.1 (2009): 115-132. Print.

Norgaard, Rolf. "Writing Information Literacy: Contributions to a Concept." *Reference and User Services Quarterly* 43.2 (Winter 2003): 124-130. Print.

———. "Writing Information Literacy in the Classroom: Pedagogical Enactments and Implications." *Reference and User Services Quarterly* 43.3 (Spring 2004): 220-226. Print.

Owusu-Ansah, Edward K. "Information Literacy and Higher Education: Placing the

Academic Library in the Center of a Comprehensive Solution." *The Journal of Academic Librarianship* 30.1 (2004): 3-16. Print.

Reitz, Joan M. *Dictionary for Library and Information Science*. Westport: Libraries Unlimited, 2004. Print.

Rockman, Ilene, and Associates. *Integrating Information Literacy into the Higher Education Curriculum: Practical Models for Transformation*. San Francisco: Jossey-Bass, 2004. Print. The Jossey-Bass Higher and Adult Educ. Ser.

Sousa, David A. *How the Brain Learns: A Classroom Teacher's Guide*. 2nd ed. Thousand Oaks: Corwin, 2001. Print.

Sult, Leslie, and Vicki Mills. "A Blended Method for Integrating Information Literacy Instruction into English Composition Classes." *Reference Services Review* 34.3 (2006): 368-388. Print.

VanderPol, Diane, Jeanne M. Brown, and Patricia Iannuzzi. "Reforming the Undergraduate Experience." *New Directions for Teaching and Learning* 114 (Summer 2008): 5-15. Print.

York, Amy C., and Jason M. Vance. "Taking Library Instruction into the Online Classroom: Best Practices for Embedded Librarians." *Journal of Library Administration* 49.1 (2009): 197-209. Print.

Appendix

Information Literacy Proficiencies for Students Ready to Move Into Upper-division Coursework

Information Literacy Articulation Group of Greater Portland - 4/10/08

Students who are ready to begin upper-division coursework can...

1. Identify gaps in their knowledge and recognize when they need information.
- Read and analyze assignments and class instructions.
- Determine the nature and extent of information needed.
- Confer with instructors, librarians, and others to focus and refine a research topic.
- Frame appropriate research questions and develop a manageable thesis statement.

2. Find information efficiently and effectively, using appropriate research tools and search strategies.
- Understand that there are different resources available for different purposes/subjects.
- Explore general information sources to increase familiarity with a topic.
- Recognize that information sources have an organizational structure and can find and use their navigational tools and access points.
- Formulate a search to locate and retrieve information effectively and efficiently using appropriate resources.
- Understand how to follow the trail from the citation to the item.
- Use the library to obtain materials including materials that aren't available locally.

3. Evaluate and select information using appropriate criteria.
- Critically evaluate information based on reliability, validity, accuracy, authority, timeliness, and point of view or bias.
- Compare and select information from various sources in order to accomplish a specific task.
- Understand that informational content and physical format are indpendent of each other.
- Judge the relevance of materials found with respect to the specific information need.

4. Treat research as a multi-stage, recursive learning process.
- Understand that information searching requires motivation, perse-

verance, and practice, and that skills are developed over time.
- Identify gaps in the information retrieved and modify or revise their topic or thesis and/or develop new search strategies.
- Formulate a realistic overall plan and timeline to acquire the needed information.

5. *Ethically and legally use information and information technologies.*
   - Cite items or ideas used and do not represent work attributable to others as your own, and do not distort the author's intended meaning.
   - Understand that citation of other works or ideas and plagiarism are ethical issues.
   - Use citations to participate in an ongoing scholarly conversation.
   - Understand that different disciplines have different citation standards and habits.
   - Understand that there are legal issues surrounding copyrighted information.

6. *Recognize safety issues involved with information sharing and information technologies.*
   - Recognize that the use of some technologies has potential health risks.
   - Recognize potential safety and privacy risks of sharing personal information online.

7. *Manipulate and manage information, using appropriate tools and technologies.*
   - Record and organize information resources to track the research process.
   - Use tools and techniques to create and revise documents collaboratively.

8. *Create, produce, and communicate understanding of a subject through synthesis of relevant information.*
   - Recognize that existing information can be combined with original thought, experimentation, and/or analysis to produce something new.
   - Analyze resources and make conscious decisions about how each resource supports the development of the topic.
   - Reconsider original idea based on new understanding.

Course Design

Writing New York: Using Google Maps as a Platform for Electronic Portfolios

Dale Jacobs, Hollie Adams, and Janine Morris

Course Description

English 302: Writing about the Arts is a practicum course offered at the University of Windsor for upper-level English undergraduate students. The course asks students to write about a variety of art forms and requires engagement with multiple genres of writing as a way for students to effectively order their experiences, reconstruct meaning in those experiences, and communicate that meaning to their readers. This version of the course involves a two-week introductory reading and writing commitment at the University of Windsor campus and then a three-week visit to New York City. In New York, the students work toward building a final portfolio using Google Maps as a showcase for their writing.

Institutional Context

The University of Windsor sits on the United States-Canada border, across from Detroit, Michigan. A comprehensive university with approximately 14,000 undergraduate and 1,600 graduate students, the University of Windsor is a compact urban campus with a large commuter population. Presently, Windsor is a city particularly challenged by the recent economic recession (especially as the downturn affects the automotive sector), with an unemployment rate of 14.3% (as of July 2009, according to Statistics Canada). Given this reality, we were unsure about the response we would receive when offering a course involving an extended field trip to New York.[1]

This particular iteration of English 302: Writing about the Arts took place during the Spring semester in 2009. The course is not mandatory for English majors, but it does satisfy departmental requirements for completing an English BA. The University of Windsor requires students earning a general English BA to complete two composition, rhetoric, linguistics, and theory courses. The majority of courses taken by English majors at the University of Windsor are literature courses, while practicum courses themselves are relatively few in number. The University of Windsor's practicum courses are designed to give students a hands-on learning experience with a smaller class size. Writing about the Arts is a regularly offered course that is usually taught on campus by Dale and, under normal circumstances, Dale has students attend and write about cultural institutions and events in the city of Windsor. However, Spring 2009's course presented students with opportunities beyond those typically granted to students in the course.

The Spring 2009 session of English 302: Writing about the Arts allowed students to move beyond the traditional classroom setting, positioning themselves within a cityscape which is much different from their own. Because of Dale's familiarity with New York City and because the city provided the necessary material for the course, Dale tried incorporating an extended field trip to New York in this term's offering. Students took Writing about the Arts in conjunction with English 376: Contemporary Drama, which also had a New York field trip component in the Spring 2009 semester. The decision to move the class outside of the city of Windsor expanded the possibilities open to students taking these courses.

Writing about the Arts came to be team taught by Dale and two graduate students, Janine and Hollie, as a result of their work together in a directed reading course, Contemporary Issues in Composition Theory, held in the 2009 Winter semester. In that course, we examined a number of trends in current Composition Theory, including the recent turn towards exploring spatial modes of meaning-making. Our readings of Nedra Reynolds, Jonathan Mauk, Richard Marback, Geoffrey Clark, and the New London Group led us to consider how we might use their ideas in the classroom. When Janine and Hollie approached Dale about the possibility of going to New York, it seemed like a perfect opportunity to put these theoretical ideas into practice.

Embracing the Council of Writing Program Administrators' guidelines, we encouraged students in this course to position themselves within an "electronic environment, to use digital technology for a multitude of purposes, [and] use electronic environments to share their texts" (Council of Writing Program Administrators). The students eventually produced a final writing portfolio on their experiences in the form of a Google Map (http://maps.google.com). We gave students certain general criteria that their maps needed to include, such as an art exhibition, a musical event, a piece of public art or architecture, a restaurant, and one arts event/place of their choice, but overall they made their decisions independently.

Before we continue, it is necessary to explain Google Maps and its use for English 302. Google Maps, in its most conventional use, is a free, Web-based virtual atlas. Through the site, users are able to control the scope of the map, from global to street level, while searching for businesses, addresses, and places of interest. Once found, such places appear as markers on the map and corresponding contact information appears in a side-bar window. Users can then select one of the locations from the side bar, prompting its marker on the map to expand to a speech bubble. The expanded marker provides users with additional information, including photos, reviews, directions, and a link to view the location at street level. For example, if you were trying to find a Starbucks Coffee in Seattle, you would type in the business name and all of the locations would pop up as place markers on a map of Seattle. From there, you can select the desired location from the sidebar or from the map itself. After making a selection, contact information, reviews, and photographs all appear on the map for that location. Similar searches can be done for other businesses, such as a restaurant, or for particular cultural institutions or landmarks, such as the Seattle Art Museum or the Space Needle. Maps of this kind can be used for planning or navigational purposes and, in fact, these are the predominant uses of Google Maps.

In 2007, Google implemented a new feature called "My Maps" to allow users to customize, annotate, and personalize their own Google Maps. Once a user creates her map (by selecting the desired location), she can add a title, description, and pre-designed place markers, each with an editable tag. The user can further customize her map by adding her own text, links, photos, and videos to the HTML tag. The user may decide to keep the map unlisted, or may make it public, including it in the Google Maps search database. It is the "My Maps" function that we incorporated into our class design and will be discussing in the remainder of this essay.

Throughout the term, students read articles from *The New Yorker* and *Time Out New York* to get a sense of published "arts" writing. In the Windsor sessions, students read previews and reviews of art exhibits, musical performances, and restaurants. For their first assignment, we asked students to collaboratively compose a Google Map prior to their trip to NYC, consisting of previews similar in nature to the writing that we assigned as mandatory reading. We assigned each student a visual arts institution and required them to choose a musical event along with one other cultural event/institution. With a class size of seventeen and now three instructors, the Windsor sessions were an ideal place to workshop students' writing, which they would then place at the appropriate locations on a collaborative Google Map. In working on this map, we asked students to seriously consider audience, purpose, context, and detail as this map was a resource for everyone who was going on the trip. Ideas about rhetoric, space, and mapping taken up through this initial activity were reinforced and considered as the term progressed.

We paid attention to the multimodal turn in the field of Composition because we wanted students to work towards a final portfolio that highlighted digital media in writing as a way to complicate the traditional written portfolio. This course was developed as way to think beyond traditional writing environments and formats as it drew on digital media to encourage students to consider the meaning of audience, context, and purpose when writing for an online, public readership. As we thought about the possibilities of using digital media, it occurred to us that Google Maps could not only provide a pre-trip resource, but also serve as a powerful platform for showcasing students' experiences of and writing about New York. Ultimately, we decided that students would collect and present their writing over the course of the term using Google Maps instead of a traditional portfolio. Students were asked to reflect on their movement throughout the city as they re-created their experience in a public forum and consider the impact of audience on a publicly accessible document. The final portfolios consisted of each student collecting his or her writing and creating an individual map, centering on a theme of his or her choice. By having students pinpoint, put into context, and make meaning of their encounters with New York, they became central in creating and re-creating the city. Each student was required to write a short introduction to his or her Google Map, engaging both the theme of the map and the act of mapping itself. The development of theme in response to the given criteria required students to think about how they were spatially positioned in the city and how their responses to the places they encountered and marked on their map could persuade and affect a public audience. By overlaying their written engagement with place on an actual map of the city, students were better able to see how their writing was shaped by their interactions with the physical place.

In New York, the class stayed at an NYU dormitory on 5th Avenue and 10th Street. From this base, the students visited museums such as the Metropolitan Museum of Art and the Museum of Modern Art, attended performances at Bargemusic and the New York Ballet, explored galleries throughout the city, and attended a large number of events on their own. The activities involved students' ability to rely on maps to navigate the city; from these experiences and these acts of mapping, students prepared writing for each class session. As a result of being placed in a new location, mapping became an essential feature of the course, not only for the day-to-day activities of the students, but as a way to think beyond the classroom and realize the importance of place in their work.

Theoretical Rationale

While we held class in a small black box theater on the second floor of our NYU residence hall, the city effectively became the classroom. We knew maps of the area would be essential for navigating the terrain of this new space, but we felt we needed to do more than simply hand students a detailed street map and send them on their way. Additionally, when it came time for the students to become mapmakers rather than map readers, we wanted to discourage them from viewing their maps as objective, accurate, transparent, or neutral, descriptors which Dennis Wood claims, "all conspire to disguise the map as a . . . *reproduction* . . . of the world, disabling us from recognizing it for a social construction" (22).

Although we would not be able to sufficiently train our English students in the theories of Cartography, still we felt it necessary to illuminate the nature of maps, empowering our students to regard them not only as wayfaring guides to be consulted but also as texts to be interpreted. Viewing maps as interpretive documents is in line with what Wood claims is their very nature: "maps, all maps, inevitably, unavoidably, necessarily embody their author's prejudices, biases and partialities (not to mention the less frequently observed art, curiosity, elegance, focus, care, imagination, attention, intelligence and scholarship their makers bring to their labor)" (24). Heeding Wood's cautionary claims about the power of maps, we felt it necessary to explore the implications of map authorship with our students.

We hoped that students would come to recognize that in producing a map they are essentially *creating* a subjective notion of space rather than *reproducing* an objective reality. Audiences often fail to consider the authorship of a map in the same ways one considers the authorship of other "written" documents. The mapmaker, much like any other author, must make choices about what to include and exclude, what argument to make, to whom the argument will be directed, and how to shape the document for that intended audience. Consequently, as J.B. Harley concludes, "all maps are *rhetorical* texts. . . . All maps employ the common devices of rhetoric such as invocation of authority. . . . Rhetoric may be concealed but it is always present" (242, emphasis added). For example, a city map in a guidebook points the reader toward certain conclusions about where to go and what to see, while a transit map offers information about public transportation routes. Both claim authority within a certain domain through the choices authors make about what to include and what to exclude. As principles of rhetoric are central to our course, the use of mapping acts as another way to reinforce these principles.

The rhetorical nature of maps grants students decision-making agency and authority as they learn to reconcile issues of purpose, audience, and context. In our case, students were required to ask themselves which larger idea about New York City they wished to convey and to whom. Through writing their Google Maps, students made choices along the way about diction, arrangement, and voice, and through the reflective writing in the introductions to their maps, students analyzed their choices. This assignment required students to distance themselves from their own texts in order to critically engage them much like they were asked to do with more traditional forms of writing about the arts (reviews from *The New Yorker*, for example).

In our attempt to forge connections between Cartography and Composition, we turned to compositionists whose work engages the rhetorical nature of space and place. We were particularly interested in Nedra Reynolds' *Geographies of Writing: Inhabiting Places and Encountering Difference,* which calls attention to the spatiality of writers' identities and the making of meaning.[2] Reynolds reminds us that geography literally means "writing the earth" and thus encourages a geographical turn in Composition Studies (51). She argues, "Geography gives us the metaphorical and methodological tools to change our ways of imagining writing through both movement and dwelling—to see writing as a set of spatial practices informed by everyday negotiations of space" (6). It only seemed fitting that we borrow Geography's tools during the relocation of our writing class from Windsor to New York, as our movement through and dwelling within the city were highlighted in ways that were taken for granted back on our home campus. Stressing the fact that all writing is geographic, we required students to write geography, to write the city of New York. On this issue, Reynolds maintains,

> Geographies of writing suggest that college students in writing classes, as agents who move through the world, know a great deal more about "writing" than they think they do—not that they are holding out on us, but that we haven't yet tapped their spatial imaginations or studied their moves. (176)

We felt that in requesting students to self-examine their movement through the city we could tap these "spatial imaginations," requiring them to do something rarely asked of them in the English department—to negotiate space and place through their writing.

We, like Reynolds, see writing as material, tied to a place and time (in this case New York City), and wanted to empower our students to see the role of materiality in how they construct meaning in their writing. We could think of no better way to do so than to have students plot their documents on a map, which then acted like a palimpsest, a visual reminder of spatiality beneath the writing etched over it. Writing virtually on the map, we hoped, would better prompt students to consider how the place they visited or the event they took part in was necessarily tied to its spatial context—to the cultural, political, or economic fabric of its surrounding neighborhood. Students were encouraged to view their experience of the city spatially, taking up Reynolds's call to attend to the *where* of writing as well as navigation, arrangement, memory, and composition—elements tied to acts of both mapping and writing. Similarly, we hoped students would begin to see how their identities as writers had been shaped in much the same way, leading to inherent biases and prejudices, not to be overcome or denied, but to be recognized and explored in their writing. Reynolds argues that teachers of writing "need to know more about the spatial practices that students bring with them and how to tap into their embodied practices—in screen culture as well as street culture—for their acts of composing, their habitats and places meaningful to them" (175). The platform of the Google Map allowed us to succinctly combine screen culture and street culture, overlaying the spatiality of writing on a map with the opportunities for multimodality embedded in composing with new media.

Cynthia Selfe defines "new media texts" as texts "primarily created in digital environments, composed in multiple media (e.g., film, video, audio, among others), and designed for the presentation and exchange in digital venues" (44). She further writes that these texts heavily value visual elements and often incorporate interactivity. The Google Maps assignment embodies Selfe's definition, as well as the ideas of the New London Group. In their work, the New London Group identifies six design elements: the linguistic, audio, visual, gestural, and spatial modes, as well as the multimodal, the combined effect of all of the preceding modes (5). Though the text of the map may have initially begun as ideas sketched in pocket notebooks as students navigated the city, the final incarnations appear solely in multimodal digital form, within the text blocks afforded by Google Maps accompanied by pictures, links, and/or video to help convey the students' multi-layered ideas about the place, providing the reader with an interactive space to navigate.

To draw attention to the importance of audience, we encouraged students to share their document in its digital venue with the public—friends or family members interested in hearing about their experience or prospective travelers to New York City. The fact that their Google Map would become part of public domain on the Internet meant they had to develop their ideas into meaningful, reader-based prose in ways that texts-for-the-teacher's-eyes-only may not promote. In this way, the map assignment addresses the recent push in Composition Studies toward making student writing public, hence less akin to writing practice.[3]

Google Maps not only allows but also encourages the use of multimodality and interaction in ways that a traditional word-processed document does not. Hypertext links can be added by simply highlighting a word, clicking a button, and entering a Web address. Images and video can easily be added to the portfolios as well, taking up the call of many in the field to not overlook visual modes of meaning-making.[4] In this regard, we were inspired by Kathleen Blake Yancey's 2004 CCCC Chair's Address, in which she champions the digital, multimodal portfolio:

> In arrangement, a digital portfolio . . . is defined by links. Because you can link externally as well as internally, and because those links are material, you have more contexts you can link to, more strata you can layer, more "you" to invent, more invention to represent. In sum, the potential of arrangement is a function of delivery, and *what and how you arrange*—which become a function of the medium you choose—*is who you invent*. (318)

Moreover, John Trimbur argues that in equating composition solely with the act of writing, we neglect "the complex delivery systems through which writing circulates" (190). The incorporation of hypertext links and images/video into the map serves to mirror the complex delivery systems and provides a less one-sided view of meaning production.

What stands out to us in both theoretical discussions and classroom practice are the ways in which mapping in general and online mapping in particular provide rhetorical possibilities that word-based texts alone do not. To some degree, the same can be said of any kind of multimodal portfolio or writing assignment, but we have come to believe that the act of online mapping as a kind of spatial network can help students to think about invention, arrangement, and delivery in new ways. As Jeff Rice writes in "Urban Mapping: A Rhetoric of the Network,"

> the power of networks comes not from the identification of certain "things" and how they connect, but from the process of connections themselves. Generalized to a "thing" like a city space or a map, the emphasis shifts from pure analysis or representation to working with the types of connections that may or may not be generated within the space's various processes. The emphasis, in other words, is rhetorical as it teaches another perspective regarding how spaces are organized, arranged, or delivered. (209)

By mapping the city space in Google Maps, students engage in the process of making connections, seeing not only how spaces are organized, but also thinking about the choices they made in their own rhetorical arrangement of such spaces.

Unfortunately, in discussions of teaching scholars often treat the spatial and the visual as mutually exclusive modes of meaning-making. While Compositionists currently laud the visual aspect of multimodality, the spatial receives much less attention. Reynolds reminds us that the medium of the map necessarily unites "screen culture and street culture" (175); while Geography is defined as "writing the earth," it is chiefly a visual discipline. In drawing from Cartography to construct our Google Maps portfolio assignment, we can encourage multimodality, especially the visual aspects, promote interactivity, and endorse public writing, while attending to the spatiality of meaning-making and ultimately retaining a focus on the writing itself.

Critical Reflection

In reflecting on our experience in teaching this class, we considered a number of questions. How did the use of Google Maps contribute to our ability to teach rhetorical ideas of composing? Did it help students engage in spatial meaning-making? Did it increase students' attention to arrangement? Were students better able to make connections between place, movement, and identity? Between visual, spatial, and linguistic practices? How did using Google Maps alter our experience as teachers and the experience of students? In thinking through these questions, we consider both the strengths and the weaknesses of this iteration of the course, focusing especially on the introductions that students wrote for their Google Maps, as these introductions provide the best lens for viewing their processes.

As students worked on their maps, we encouraged them to make connections between the five sites they were expected to include in ways that would help them understand how their maps serve as rhetorical, public documents. Connective themes, such as bodies in performance, fusion, modernity, communication, popular culture, artistic interpretation, and serendipity emerged from these projects, working to greater or lesser degrees to help students think through their interactions with New York City as a space and their maps as representations of their experiences in that space. For example, one student, Hope Marion, who was initially intimidated by the idea of New York, used the project to work through the themes of communication and connection. For her, the mapping project reinforced the ways in which the idea of spatiality is crucial to the way we make meaning, especially as we encounter a new place. Through the Google Maps project, Hope[5] was able to make connections between place, movement, and identity in ways that she had not anticipated prior to composing her map. In her introduction she writes,

I had never been to New York City, and was intimidated by my impressions of it. Descriptions of New York to those outside the city often paint a picture of a city so massive that anything personal is entirely lost. It is also often depicted as a highly uncommunicative city, in which individuals are so wrapped up in their own lives that there is little sense of community. My experience of New York counteracted all of these impressions. I found that all around me was evidence of people striving to connect with others. The New Yorkers I spoke to were all friendly and more than willing to give me a moment of their time to provide directions, or even make suggestions about what to see and do while in the city. While this map does not include those people, I hope that the overall impression left is one of welcome and inclusiveness. The map is restricted to Manhattan solely due to my limited travels outside of that part of the city. I wonder how much my experience would have differed in different areas. I also hope this map serves to "shrink" New York to a certain extent. One of the major factors that intimidated me about the city was its sheer size. The truth is, while New York is massive, it is not possible to grasp the scale of the city at street (or subway) level. It is only possible to experience a few blocks of the city at any given time, which is just as it should be. By citing the locations I have chosen, largely in Greenwich Village, I hope to draw attention to the smaller communities that exist within the gargantuan metropolis that is New York City. (1)

In this case, the map facilitates her theme, helping her to make the city more manageable for her and her readers; for Hope, the spatial representation of the city aids in the creation of both meaning and identity.

For Hope, like many of our students, working with Google Maps made New York City manageable in scope, both as they experienced it and as they represented it. The main reason for this feeling, expressed by a number of students, is related to the ways in which users (both readers and writers) of Google Maps can control/customize how they interact with digital space. As Shauna Pellow describes in her introduction,

> The visual display of the Google Map allows the user to see New York City in a way that is not overwhelming, as the city is usually viewed. The context of this map allows me to zoom in to the particular area I have marked, and place a pin in the location of each of the events. As a result, users are able to view more information at their leisure, instead of feeling flooded with all material at once. This is particularly useful as [the] point of my map is to help the audience view New York City as a smaller, communal city, instead of a large and overwhelming metropolis. The layout and features of Google Map help to humanize the tool of a map, and in this case, to humanize New York City. (1)

In other words, it's not just the act of putting together a writing portfolio or the act of mapping that led students to the kinds of observations that Shauna and Hope depict, but rather it's the particular confluence of writing on the Google Map platform, using its customizable features that allows for this private-public spatial meaning to occur.

Of course, not all students were able to see how the act of mapping and the use of the spatial helped them create meaning, nor how the features of Google Maps helped them convey their ideas to an intended audience. For these students, the written text they produced was only marginally connected to the map and the multimodal possibilities remained unexplored; to a large extent, Google Maps simply acted as a folder for their writing. The most successful students not only demonstrated an increased awareness of spatial meaning-making, but also rhetorical ideas of invention, arrangement, and delivery in their final Google Maps projects. One example is Justin Quenneville, who took inspiration from Bob Dylan in titling his map "Modern Gomorrah." In his introduction he writes,

> Thinking about my work and the city as a large Google Map made me appreciate the space I covered and see New York as one grand work of art. Using a map not as reference point but as canvas really makes this portfolio project come to life because my work becomes part of the city's landscape. Placing my articles down exactly where they belong makes them more real in my own mind. . . . It exists as a fluid and functioning

whole with all the pieces, no matter how Godless or sacred, as a beautiful machine. (1)

As with Shauna and Hope, the act of mapping forced Justin to think spatially and make connections in ways he might not otherwise have made them. The Google Maps assignment did not just exist on the computer screen but informed Justin's experience of the city itself and, like Hope's map, made it more manageable. However, Justin's writing, both in his introduction and on his map, is not confined to writer-based prose, but embodies a concern for public writing. This identification of writing as a public act can be seen even more fully in Cristina's work.

Cristina Naccarato whose map is entitled "D.I.Y. New York City," writes in her introduction that

> The use of a map helped me to contextualize the space of the map I used, versus the actual spaces that I wrote about. In a sense, by placing these points on a map, rather than writing about them on a blog or in a book, I'm visually creating a space for my reader/viewer where they can interpret the framework I wrote about. (1)

Cristina, even more explicitly than the other students, sees the use of Google Maps as a rhetorical endeavor. Her attention to rhetorical ideas such as audience is evident in her reference to her map as a space created specifically for her reader/viewer, as well as in her map's cohesiveness. The relatively "underground" sites she reviews are consistent with her map's theme of exploring the D.I.Y. (Do-It-Yourself) aesthetic currently thriving in New York. In choosing sites that are emblematic of radical counter-culture, her writing is consistently aware of its potential audience beyond that of her instructor.

Cristina recognizes that those who would be interested in "D.I.Y. New York City" are likely young adults, avid listeners of music beyond Top 40 rotation, enthusiasts of non-commercial art, sympathizers to a vegetarian or vegan lifestyle, and those who are familiar with such terms as "hipster" and "indie" (not to mention "D.I.Y."). Reviewing Hillstock, a permit-less rooftop music festival in Brooklyn, she directly addresses this particular audience: "Mixing a wide variety of underground artists, any fan of non-commercial music would be able to find something they could bob their head to or hum along with. From indie, to punk, to pop, to ska, to electronic, you name it, chances are, you could find it at this fest" ("D.I.Y. New York City: Hillstock," par. 2). Likewise, when writing about The Renegade Craft Fair, she makes similar assumptions of her reader:

> At the fair, you'll be sure to find tons of cute and original pieces, ranging from homemade knitted, reconstructed, stenciled and hand sewn clothing, hand-made and designed jewelry, vintage treasures and other knick

knacks you'll never be able to find anywhere else. With 300+ vendors and artists, there's sure to be an original piece screaming your name. ("D.I.Y. New York City: The Renegade Craft Fair," par. 2)

In making such assumptions and tailoring her writing appropriately, Cristina's portfolio successfully moves beyond mere personal writer-based reflection to a more meaningful reader-based prose as it becomes a useful public resource for those interested in seeking out New York City's counterculture. Not only is the writing strong, but also her map is aesthetically pleasing, inviting readership and interactivity.

With an abundance of relevant photographs, images, and hypertext links, Cristina's map makes meaning beyond the textual level. Her map builds on the best aspects of multimodal portfolios, moving into the sphere of public writing and emphasizing the spatial as a mode of meaning-making. Christina's map exemplifies the ways in which we, as instructors, strived to situate rhetorical ideas of invention, arrangement, and delivery at the forefront of our course and our assignments.

Not all students were able to make such complex connections or use Google Maps to produce effective public writing; for example, some portfolios read more like personal travel journals, without any clear overarching purpose or sense of audience. One of the ways we would attempt to address this issue in the future is to use the collaborative Google Map as a better scaffold to the final Google Maps project in order to help students see how meaning can be made spatially and that Google Maps can be a rhetorical tool. In retrospect, we should have enabled and encouraged comments on the collaborative map, resulting in greater collaboration before, during, and after the trip so that while students were making sense of their experience, they could represent that experience collaboratively. In addition, we would also spend even more time in class addressing the idea of mapping as a rhetorical act. We would perhaps have students read some introductory material on mapping and examine maps with an eye to their rhetorical construction. Now that we have a collection of sample material from the Spring 2009 class, such work could extend to a new semester's examination of previous Google Maps as a way to show both rhetorical strategies and the multimodal possibilities inherent in the use of Google Maps.

Of course, teaching a course with an extensive field trip component is rarely an option. How, then, could this idea of using Google Maps as a writing platform be adapted to courses taught at one's home institution? A number of ideas come to mind. In teaching the Writing about the Arts course described here without a field trip component, Google Maps would still be an effective way to have students think through issues of space as they move through the Windsor-Detroit area, engaging with various types of art and art events. In this case, Windsor-Detroit (rather than NYC) becomes the spatial locus of their experiences, and their mapping of it becomes a way to think through their subjective senses of that space. Another such themed course could focus on the city of Windsor itself, requiring students to write in a mix of genres such as profiles, historical vignettes, opinion pieces, and proposals for change as a way to represent and make meaning from the city. Combined with photographs, video, and the other possibilities within Google Maps, students could create a rich portrait of the city in which they live and study. Maps of this kind could be used as a way to inform members and prospective members of the community, contributing to public dialogue, and possibly inspiring change within a community. Both of these course ideas could be adapted to any region/city either as full courses or as one segment of a larger course; these are just two of the many possibilities afforded by Google Maps as a writing platform. In any case, writing of this kind would push students to begin to think more about the ways in which they create meaning from the spaces around them.

As teachers, we learned a great deal about the possibilities that exist in using Google Maps as a platform for final portfolios. Before this course, the three of us had read the work of Reynolds, Mauk, Marback, Clark, and the New London Group and talked about the ways in which the spatial was an overlooked mode of meaning-making in the composition classroom, but it wasn't until we taught this course that we really understood the full implications of these ideas as they filtered through student experience. Additionally, we came to appreciate the rhetorical possibilities for students in producing this kind of text. While we realize that the extended field trip made this particular course unusual, we see the potential for using mapping and Google Maps in future courses that do not have a travel component (such as mapping one's own campus or city) but that nonetheless ask students to pay attention to their surroundings and make spatial meaning from them.

Notes

1 In addition to tuition and transportation costs, the course required students to pay a fee of $1,900 to cover room, board, and admissions to all required events/outings. Unfortunately, no funding was available for students to further defray these costs.
2 For more on these connections, see also Mauk, Clark, and Marback.
3 See Weisser for an in-depth analysis of public writing.
4 See Hayles, Haas, Rice, Shipka, and Wysocki for additional ways that the visual mode can be incorporated into the composition classroom.
5 The final student Google Maps can be viewed at the following URLs:

Hope Marion <http://maps.google.ca/maps/ms?hl=en&ie=UTF8&msa=0&msid=100988966170789336776.00046d1214c8d4d8de8f4&ll=40.761431,-73.966999&spn=0.043687,0.093727&z=13>

Cristina Naccarato <http://maps.google.ca/maps/ms?ie=UTF8&hl=e
n&msa=0&msid=106101561373386268305.00046d0e04ad84ddd2845&
ll=40.683762,-73.858337&spn=0.144754,0.307961&z=12>

Shauna Pellow <http://maps.google.com/maps/ms?ie=UTF8&hl=e
n&msa=0&msid=103183357056614029047.00046cf3fe9e70c3c8435&
ll=40.840308,-73.931808&spn=0.126751,0.30899&z=12>

Justin Quenneville <http://maps.google.com/maps/ms?ie=UTF8&msa=0
&msid=118433904883706129242.00046cf0a66bcccaad9d6&z=12>

Works Cited

Clark, Gregory. "Writing as Travel, or Rhetoric on the Road." *CCC* 49.1 (1998): 9-23. Print.

Council of Writing Program Administrators. *WPA Outcomes Statement for First Year Composition*, 2005-2009. Web. 29 July 2009.

Haas, Christina. *Writing Technology: Studies on the Materiality of Literacy*. Mahwah: Lawrence Erlbaum, 1996. Print.

Harley, J.B. "Deconstructing the Map." *Writing Worlds: Discourse, Text and Metaphor in the Representation of Landscape*. Ed. Trevor Barnes and James Duncan. New York: Routledge, 1991. 231-247. Print.

Hayles, Katherine. *Writing Machines*. Cambridge: MIT, 2002. Print.

Marback, Richard. "Detroit and the Closed Fist: Toward a Theory of Material Rhetoric." *Rhetoric Review* 17.1 (1998): 74-90. Print.

Marion, Hope. "Introduction to Final Project." 2009. TS. University of Windsor, Writing about the Arts, New York/Windsor.

———. *Final Project. Google Maps*. 23 June 2009. Web. 29 July 2009.

Mauk, Johnathon. "Location, Location, Location: The 'Real' (E)states of Being, Writing, and Thinking in Composition." *College English* 65.4 (2003): 368-388. Print.

Naccarato, Cristina. "D.I.Y. New York City: Hillstock." *D.I.Y. New York City. Google Maps*. 23 June 2009. Web. 29 July 2009.

———. "D.I.Y. New York City: The Renegade Craft Fair." *D.I.Y. New York City. Google Maps*. 23 June 2009. Web. 29 July 2009.

———. "Introduction to D.I.Y. New York City." 2009. TS. University of Windsor, Writing about the Arts, New York/Windsor.

New London Group. "A Pedagogy of Multiliteracies: Designing Social Futures." *Multiliteracies: Literacy Learning and the Design of Social Futures*. Ed. Bill Cope and M. Kalantzis. New York: Routledge, 2000. 9-37. Print.

Pellow, Shauna. *Come Together NYC. Google Maps*. 22 June 2009. Web. 29 July 2009.

———. "Introduction to Come Together NYC." *Google Maps*. 2009. TS. University of Windsor, Writing about the Arts, New York/Windsor.

Quenneville, Justin. "Introduction to Modern Gomorrah." 2009. TS. University of Windsor, Writing about the Arts, New York/Windsor.

———. *Modern Gomorrah. Google Maps*. 22 June 2009. Web. 29 July 2009.

Reynolds, Nedra. *Geographies of Writing: Inhabiting Places and Encountering Difference.* Carbondale: Southern Illinois UP, 2007. Print.

Rice, Jeff. "Urban Mapping: A Rhetoric of the Network." *Rhetoric Society Quarterly* 38.2 (2008): 198-218. Print.

Selfe, Cynthia L. "Students Who Teach Us: A Case Study of A New Media Text Designer." *Writing New Media: Theory and Applications for Expanding the Teaching of Composition.* Ed. Anne Frances Wysocki, Johndan Johnson-Eilola, Cynthia L. Selfe, and Geoffrey Sirc. Logan: Utah State UP, 2004. 43-66. Print.

Shipka, Jody. "A Multimodal Task-Based Framework for Composing." *CCC* 57.2 (2005): 277-306. Print.

Statistics Canada. *Labour force characteristics, unadjusted, by census metropolitan area (3 month moving average). Summary Tables.* 13 July 2009. Web. 29 July 2009.

Trimbur, John. "Composition and the Circulation of Writing." *CCC* 52.2 (2000): 188-219. Print.

Weisser, Christian. *Moving beyond Academic Discourse: Composition Studies and the Public Sphere.* Carbondale: Southern Illinois UP, 2002. Print.

Wood, Dennis. *The Power of Maps.* New York: Guilford, 1992. Print.

Wysocki, Anne. "Impossibly Distinct: On Form/Content and Word/Image in Two Pieces of Computer-Based Multimedia." *Computers and Composition* 18.2 (2001): 137-162. Print.

Yancey, Kathleen Blake. "Made Not Only in Words: Composition in a New Key." *CCC* 56.2 (2004): 297-328. Print.

Syllabus

English 26-302
Writing about the Arts
Dr. Dale Jacobs

Writing about music is like dancing about architecture.
—Variously attributed to Laurie Anderson, Tom Stoppard, and/or
Steve Martin

Course Description

Writing about the arts is a difficult project that involves the translation of one medium of expression into another. It involves the ordering of our experiences, the (re)construction of meaning in those experiences, and the communication of that meaning to readers. It is difficult, but rewarding work that involves slowing down, attending to detail, and carefully watching and listening as you engage with a variety of art forms. In engaging these diverse art forms, you will use writing as a way to explore connections between art and your own lived experiences and between art and its social and cultural contexts (including the immediate context of New York). Over the course of the semester, we will write about various art forms and read current and recent magazine articles in order to think about a variety of approaches to writing about the arts. In this course, I will encourage you to be creative, to try out new techniques and approaches, and to stretch yourselves as writers. I will encourage you to engage with a number of different art forms and write in a variety of styles and genres; we will concentrate on thinking about purposes, audiences, and the contexts for your writing. This course will provide you with many opportunities to interact with each other and with me as we form a community of writers and readers engaged in thinking about the arts. I hope that in questioning, exploring and working together, we will become better writers and readers and that we will be better able to engage with and write about the arts.

Course Texts

In Windsor:
Course Handouts (Available from Heather Patterson)
The New Yorker

In New York:
The New Yorker

The Village Voice
Time Out New York
New York Magazine

Be active readers. Do not read for information only, but instead think about what approaches the writers are using, how they have structured their pieces, how they have envisioned purpose, audience, and context, etc. In other words, read with an eye towards how it might help your own writing.

Course Requirements

Contribution to Collaborative Google Map (20%) – Each of you will contribute to a collaborative Google Map before we go to New York (I will send you an invitation in the next couple of days); the map will then serve as a resource for everyone as they plan their activities. I encourage you to begin your research as soon as possible. There are plenty of resources to help you begin thinking about what's going on, including (but certainly not limited to) *The New Yorker*, *The New York Times* (online at www.nytimes.com and through electronic subscription at Leddy), *Time Out New York* online (newyork.timeout.com), *Village Voice* online (www.villagevoice.com), *New York Magazine* online (nymag.com), Pollstar (pollstar.com), and Metromix (newyork.metromix.com). Guidebooks are also a good source as you begin your research (Chapters will have a good selection of NYC guides, as will Windsor Public Library).

This assignment has three (3) parts.

(1) I have assigned each of you a visual arts institution (see list below). For your assigned institution, you will write a 750-1,000 word entry that will be embedded on the map at the appropriate location (the pins have already been placed). Provide context (historical, geographical, cultural, etc.) for the institution so that your readers will understand how it fits into the cultural fabric of New York as a city and/or the art world as a whole. As well, provide a description of the major exhibitions currently on display. Remember that you are providing a resource.

(2) Pick a musical event (any genre) and mark it on the map with a light blue marker (click on icon and it will give you a list of options); in the title, include the names of the artist and venue, as well as your name. Write a 500-750 word entry in which you try to convince your classmates to attend this event. Provide background context for both the venue and the artist.

(3) Pick any other arts event/institution (dance, theater, film, music, visual art, performing art, food, etc.) and mark it on the map with a red marker with a black dot (click on icon and it will give you a list of options). Write a 250-500 word entry in which you try to convince your classmates to attend this event/institution. Provide contextual information.

Due by 9 a.m., Monday, May 18, 2009.

Visual Arts Institutions

New Museum of Contemporary Art
Morgan Library & Museum
Neue Gallerie New York
Fashion Institute of Technology: The Museum at FIT
Guggenheim Museum
The Cloisters
Cooper-Hewitt Museum
International Center for Photography
Whitney Museum of American Art
Frick Collection
Brooklyn Museum of Art
Museum of Arts & Design
American Folk Art Museum
P.S. 1 Contemporary Art Center
Jewish Museum
Studio Museum Harlem
Bronx Museum of the Arts

Panel Discussion (10%) – While in New York, each of you will be part of a group that will lead class discussion. Each group will lead class on one of the following activities: Visit to the Metropolitan Museum of Art; Liz Magnes at Bargemusic; Visit to the Museum of Modern Art; New York City Ballet performance. Each group (4-5 people per group) will give a 15-minute presentation designed to get everyone thinking about the specific experience. Your group presentation should include any observations your group wants to make about the event, questions you want to discuss about the event, and questions/activities designed to help us think about writing about this event. The presentation is designed to set up the subsequent discussion period and will lead into a 45-minute discussion that your group will facilitate.

Final Portfolio/Individual Google Map (50%) – The final portfolio for this course will be in the form of an individual Google Map. On this map, you must include writing/entries on the following events of your choosing:

Art exhibition; Musical event; Architecture or piece of public art; Restaurant; One other event/site of your choice. Each of these entries can be up to 1,200 words (the maximum for a Google map entry); remember that you should be concentrating on providing both context and detail for your entries. As well, you can include photographs and video as part of your map. You should also include a 3-4 page introduction in which you show how this map works as a coherent whole. Explain what you are trying to do with this project. Who is your audience? What is your purpose? How does the context of mapping affect the way you put this project together? If you have included photos and/or video, how does it fit into the overall project of your map? The URL for your map and your introduction (a Word file with a .doc or .rtf extension) should be emailed to djacobs@uwindsor.ca.

Due by 9 a.m. on Wednesday, June 24, 2009.

Class Participation and Attendance (20%) – Every member of the class is important and so everyone will be expected to attend all classes and participate fully in class activities, including peer response, writing activities, field trip activities, and discussion.

Grade Distribution
Contribution to Collaborative Google Map	20%
Panel Discussion	10%
Final Portfolio/Individual Google Map	50%
Class Participation and Attendance	20%

Late assignments will be penalized 1/3 letter grade per day. If an unavoidable problem arises, talk to me before the due date.

*The **Writing Lab Newsletter*** (WLN) is a bi-monthly publication (September to June) for those who work in the tutorial setting of writing labs or centers (or in writing centers within learning centers). Articles focus on writing center theory, administration, and pedagogy. The website, http://writinglabnewsletter.org, contains an open archive of past volumes.

Call for Papers: WLN invites articles, reviews of books relevant to writing centers, and revisions of papers presented at regional conferences. We also regularly include a Tutors' Column with essays by and for tutors. Recommended maximum length is 3000 words or less (including the Works Cited) for articles and 1500 words or less for the Tutors' Column. Please use MLA format. All submissions are peer reviewed. Send your manuscripts as attachments via e-mail to submission@writinglabnewsletter.org. For editorial questions, contact Muriel Harris (harrism@purdue.edu), Editor, or Michael Mattison (mmattison@wittenberg.edu) or Janet Auten (jauten@american.edu), Associate Editor.

Subscriptions to WLN are U.S. $25 per year for subscriptions mailed in the U.S. and U.S. $30 for subscriptions mailed to Canada. International and digital subscriptions are also available by contacting support@therichco.com. Please order WLN through our Web site: <http://writinglabnewsletter.org/index.html>

Rhetorica in Motion: Feminist Methods and Methodologies, edited by Eileen K. Schell and K.J. Rawson. Pittsburgh: U of Pittsburgh P, 2010. 232 pp.

Reviewed by Wendy Sharer, East Carolina University

This is an ambitious collection, and its breadth makes it an excellent resource for those new to feminist rhetorical studies. I was not surprised to learn, as Eileen Schell explains in her introduction, that the book grew out of a graduate seminar. While the essays span a variety of topics, several common goals hold them together: challenging the coercive forces of "normality"; recognizing and celebrating the embodied nature of experience; and prioritizing ethical engagement with the subjects of research. As the title of the collection suggests, the majority of the chapters address research issues in rhetorical studies and thus do not offer direct insights for the writing classroom; however, many of the methods and methodologies discussed draw on the kinds of critical reading and writing practices many of us foster in our composition classrooms. In fact, the final chapter of the collection is a "Pedagogical Postscript" that, as elaborated below, provides excellent insights and practical suggestions for how feminist research methods and methodologies can enrich writing instruction.

The first part of the collection, "Theoretical and Methodological Challenges," includes four pieces that explore ways to expand the work that feminist scholars have already done in rhetorical studies. Jay Dolmage and Cynthia Lewiecki-Wilson identify parallels between feminism and disability studies. As feminist historians of Rhetoric and Composition have challenged models that position male bodies at the heart of the rhetorical tradition, so too have scholars in disability studies undermined the assumption that one type of body is normal or naturally superior to others. As feminist theorists have questioned the passive positioning of female research subjects, so too have disability theorists challenged the passive positioning of disabled bodies in research. Feminists and disability studies scholars also share the goal of critiquing normative terminology. Feminists have exposed the essentializing potential of the category "woman," just as scholars of disability studies have worked to reveal the complex identities traditionally lumped together within the category of the "disabled." Dolmage and Lewiecki-Wilson urge further collaboration between feminists and scholars of disability studies within Rhetoric as both groups seek to "read against the practices that produce normalizing categories of all kinds" (38).

In "Queering Feminist Rhetorical Canonization," K.J. Rawson continues the discussion of feminist challenges to normative categories by calling for work that complicates the male/female binary that has informed much feminist historical work in Rhetoric. To trouble this persistent binary, Rawson uses "transgender critique," an application of queer theory. Rather than using the categories "female" or "woman," Rawson recommends that feminist scholars explore rhetorical history through the lens—and the multiple, shifting meanings—of gender.

Concerns about unquestioned privilege also inform Wendy Hesford's critique of Western bias in feminist rhetorical scholarship. Because Western feminists tend to be the ones who have the freedom and capital to travel, they tend to be the ones who represent the conditions of other women's lives around the globe. To counter the tradition of Western bias in international feminism, Hesford calls for the development of "a transnational feminist analytic" that "reads across contexts and focuses particular attention on how arguments travel across cultural and national borders" (62). Such an analytical framework would keep feminist scholars attuned to conditions that might allow for only certain viewpoints to circulate.

Ilene Crawford's study of literacy practices among contemporary Vietnamese women illustrates the importance of the kind of "transnational feminist analytic" that Hesford calls for. While Western views of Vietnam lead to readings of that society through the legacy of the Vietnam War, Crawford's research suggests that the rhetorical practices of Vietnamese women are much more influenced by technologies and economies of the twenty-first century than they are by Vietnam's turbulent past. Crawford's work aims to displace the "codified images and terms" that mass media and popular discourse have placed in the forefront of Western approaches to Vietnam (72).

The second part of the collection, "Reflective Applications," provides what its name promises: detailed examples of applied feminist rhetorical methods. Kathleen Ryan describes a "feminist pragmatic rhetoric"—a collection of research practices emphasizing "situated knowledge making and acting in the world to better the world" (90)—that she has used in her previous work, and, later in the section, Joanne Addison explores ways that feminist empirical researchers can practice "strong objectivity"—a concept drawn from feminist standpoint theory that suggests that a researcher should gather various perspectives on a problem in order to put those perspectives into conversation to reach rich, although never definitive or truly objective, conclusions. One method to employ in the service of strong objectivity, Addison explains, is "experience sampling," "a technique that allows researchers to gather real-time data about what a specified group of people is doing and how those people feel about what they are doing within everyday settings" (145).

In a chapter that blends discussion of methodology and method, clearly echoing some of the conversations in Part 1 of the collection, Bernadette

Calafell explains how she has created what she calls "a homeplace" within the academy by actively engaging her identity in her research methods. Drawing on Gloria Anzaldua, Cherrie Moraga, bell hooks, and others, Calafell explains the importance of feminist methods that embrace the identity struggles women of color face when attempting to enter academic conversations, conversations that have long privileged distance and disengagement from embodied experience. Effacing the body in research practices, Calafell emphasizes, leaves unexplored the dominant position of the white, male, heterosexual body in academic research.

Ethical issues surrounding feminist research methods also receive significant attention in Part 2. Frances Ranney's chapter, for example, details a dilemma she faced when researching an organization that assisted once-wealthy women who found themselves in need of financial assistance during the Great Depression. In exploring the organization's archives, Ranney and her co-researchers discovered files detailing the case of "Fontia R." Although the discourses of conspicuous consumption and eugenics that inform Fontia R.'s situation are fascinating, Ranney hesitates to tell Fontia R.'s story because doing so does not seem to be in keeping with a feminist "ethic of care" for the research subject (124). To address this dilemma, Ranney puts forth a research method she calls "imagin-activation," a way of reading archival materials that, as Gwen Gorzelsky explains in a lucid response to Ranney's rather complex chapter, puts those materials and the people who produced them into conversation with "culturally constructed images, perceptions, beliefs, and investments," so that archival research becomes less about discussing the actions and beliefs of individuals and more about analyzing how those actions and beliefs come to be and come to be known through cultural constructs.

Heidi McKee and James Porter also address ethical concerns of feminist researchers. More specifically, they examine the work of three researchers who study interactions in online groups. Drawing on the research practices of these scholars, McKee and Porter identify six characteristics of ethical feminist research: a commitment to social justice and improvement of the circumstances for the participants; careful and respectful treatment of research participants; critically reflexive use of research methods; flexibility in identifying and carrying out research projects; dialogic approaches, such as inviting participants to "join in the decision-making process" of the research; and transparency, or a willingness "to acknowledge and make visible the complexities of the process of research" (170).

McKee and Porter note that, in interviewing two of the three researchers they studied, "neither researcher explicitly mentioned their views as informed by 'feminist research.' Rather, both researchers articulated their positions in terms of the criteria for good research in general" (166). Indeed, this articulation seems to be true about the methods and methodologies discussed throughout the collection—these are feminist research practices, but they are also good research practices in general because they address some of the troubling aspects of "traditional" research methods. Feminist research methods, like the feminist methodologies they grow out of, challenge the norms of research practice so that privilege and omissions performed within those norms of practice might be exposed and undermined.

The collection concludes with a "Pedagogical Postscript," an engaging exploration of how feminist rhetorical methods and methodologies might influence the teaching of writing. Laura Micciche explains how the concept of play, as constructed in the work of Donna Haraway, might inform a feminist writing pedagogy. Play has immense potential for writing instruction because it is a means by which writers foster "intentional ambiguity," or spaces where meanings are troubled, unsettled, created, and recreated (175). Interestingly, "play," as Micciche describes it, is reminiscent of the feminist rhetorical methods and methodologies discussed earlier in the collection, methods and methodologies aimed at problematizing the "normal" and troubling binaries. When the "normal" is undermined and when the spaces between the dichotomous poles are inhabited through play, feminist researchers can discover new and important meanings. Micciche asks readers to consider the benefits of asking students to try similar strategies. She suggests that writing instructors integrate more opportunities for students to, as feminists do, use interruption as a political tool, employ fiction strategically in critical writing and engage the affective, embodied aspects of writing. The chapter closes with sample assignments designed to promote play in the writing classroom, and fulfills Micciche's goal of "describ[ing] ways of *doing* feminist rhetorics in writing courses" (184).

Rhetorica in Motion covers an incredible span of methods and methodologies, but it does so in a way that allows the reader to make connections across them all and to envision an ethical but productively troubling journey for feminist rhetorical studies in the future.

Greenville, NC

Vision, Rhetoric, and Social Action in the Composition Classroom, by Kristie S. Fleckenstein. Carbondale: Southern Illinois UP, 2009.

Reviewed by Keith Rhodes, Grand Valley State University

Vision, Rhetoric, and Social Action in the Composition Classroom (Vision) is a compelling work, both in content and approach. The title plainly describes the content, even if the richness with which Kristie Fleckenstein connects those terms may surprise many readers. Fleckenstein profoundly reorders our thinking about visual rhetoric, rhetoric more generally, social action in composition pedagogy, and the work of composition classrooms. Yet she does so in an engaging way, writing in restrained and personal tones and omitting some of the background discussion of theory and scholarship that a more normally pedantic work would include. This omission of extended literature review is not in the nature of failing to give credit. Instead, Fleckenstein takes responsibility for persuading us of matters with her own discussion and evidence, particularly in areas where her earlier work already provides the references we might want for further study. In substance, she writes as a more modest peer of Suzanne K. Langer, James Hillman, Jerome Bruner and others referenced more often in her earlier work on these topics; yet Fleckenstein has come into her own authoritative stance in ways that also escape those sources. Ultimately, the power of her intellectual shaping becomes an integral and essential part of her persuasive appeal—"essential" in both senses, both necessary to her case and of a piece with it.

Fleckenstein's claim is dauntingly complex. Put too simply, Fleckenstein argues that the successful composition classroom necessarily requires a melding, or "symbiotic knot," of vision, rhetoric, and social action. Her continuing metaphor of dynamic "symbiotic knots" unifying the strands of classroom situations purposefully transcends the merely aesthetic aspect of metaphor, eventually becoming almost as real as the physical circumstances represented by those knots, which are illustrated graphically in key places in the book, their mutually supportive components labeled on the threads of the knots. If the symbiotic knot is the *stasis* of Fleckenstein's project, the moving principle is a consistent assumption of hope—in the profound sense which hope is often used by pragmatically influenced philosophers like Langer and Cornell West and pragmatically informed activists like Paulo Freire and bell hooks. Fleckenstein's hope-fueled passage leads us through three stages of rhetorical symbiotic knots relevant to composition classrooms: the knots of silence, of bodies, and of contradiction. Each knot has as its archetype the fundamental knot of social action, composed of visual habit, rhetorical habit, and place. Fleckenstein claims and demonstrates that the knots of embodiment and contradiction offer ways to undo the knot of silence constructed by default pedagogies, destabilizing silencing constructs of place, vision, and rhetoric that offer students no true agency, and thereby opening up the transformative power of "agenic invention."

Vision precisely and clearly details everything outlined above as Fleckenstein unfolds her discussion. We have the expected benefit of Fleckenstein's well-crafted written style, complex constructions arranged for clarity and a broad vocabulary expertly used. By leaving aside extensive unpacking of the philosophy, politics and psychology that she has explained elsewhere, Fleckenstein opens up the potential to illustrate her thinking in sensory terms, including in each section stories drawn from her experience as a parent and a teacher of young writers, analyzing the experience of these young learners who strive for greater rhetorical agency in the places around them. The result is a book that draws readers through its challenging agenda like a good river guide would lead us through a course of difficult rapids.

The question then becomes whether the argument changes our views. As to the most obvious parts of the claim, it certainly should. Though I intentionally situated myself as a skeptical reader, I could manage no real resistance to being persuaded that composition teachers need to include more and better uses of visual pedagogy and visual components in composition projects. Similarly, Fleckenstein's analyses of location and embodiment in the composition classroom had me jumping over to my syllabi for next fall and shamefacedly revising my plans. *Vision* has already become the single book I would seek to put in the hands of anyone who needs further persuasion about why writing assignments need to have students work beyond the printed page and the seated desk, and why writing tasks need to move outside the confines of the classroom and professor's office. In a portion that I think of as the true heart of the book, subtitled "Thread 3: A Lively Classroom," Fleckenstein illustrates the story of an educational observer becoming drawn into the activity of "TeenStreet," a learning program based on street theater activities. The powerful subthemes of embodied agency and experiential learning leap from being the abstractions I must use in this short treatment to become virtual and holistic embodiments of Fleckenstein's argument. As the TeenStreet observer becomes increasingly engaged in the activities, moving from analyzing them to taking part in them, the reader of *Vision* also becomes drawn into the reality that Fleckenstein's points are to be used, not just understood.

The skeptical reader could not be overcome entirely, however. I am not yet convinced that social action is a necessary part of the puzzle created by Fleckenstein's symbiotic knots. Despite knowing where else in her work to go for answers, I find myself unable to locate Fleckenstein's philosophy within this text. As a result, I could not see on what basis readers would be expected to accept the necessity of social action as part of composition pedagogy. Among other strands, Fleckenstein presents us with threads of Martha Nussbaum's classicism, Katherine Hayles' post-structuralism, several social activist's dialectical materialism, and a few more materialist psychologists' findings on matters like empathy. She also frequently adds to a relatively thick, if often compressed, cord of American pragmatism—the latter particularly prominent in her views on language and the role of hope in forming theories for action. Indeed, if I were to attempt to read a philosophy onto *Vision* to reconcile these contending viewpoints, I would select a reading together of Susanne K. Langer's *Philosophy in a New Key* and Ann E. Berthoff's *Mysterious Barricades*, particularly since I know that

Fleckenstein has done thorough readings of Langer in the past and writes so consistently with Berthoff's pragmatist ideas about language, embodiment, and experience.

Yet though I can intuit something of the underlying argument for social action as a part of the grand symbiotic knot, I do not find that Fleckenstein presents this part of the puzzle convincingly in the book itself. Social action is a wonderful thing, and Fleckenstein is surely right in pointing out that a composition pedagogy of social action could instill a powerful and pedagogically effective level of agency and invention. I simply find no way to conclude that social action in the composition classroom has the same compelling necessity as the other parts of her vision. I think I can imagine other ways to instill a genuine sense of agency—and in fact Fleckenstein's invaluable thinking about vision, embodiment, and place helps me do that better. I find no real help in sorting out what to do about students who pursue abhorrent social action—something that will be chosen, if for fun at the professor's expense if for no better reason, by at least some students out of the thousands in my composition program each year. I find insufficient answers for those parents who will call, asking what possible pedagogical reason teacher Z might have for (from their viewpoint) requiring first-year students to support liberal social causes at the price of a grade.

Considered as a whole, *Vision, Rhetoric and Social Action in the Composition Classroom* adds considerable new weight to important discussions in composition and rhetoric. The framework of "symbiotic knots" will become a durable part of my own thinking, and would advance scholarship in our field should it become a widely-shared way of discussing these themes—as it should. Fleckenstein's scholarship and thinking about vision, embodiment, location, and agency will educate and delight anyone interested in rhetoric and composition classrooms. Indeed, I do not find that I can reject what Fleckenstein claims about the role of social action, either. Instead, I want to know more, and mainly want to have her connect much of her earlier work more fully with that theme. That is, *Vision* has done quite enough work for one book to do. I am simply greedily interested in having Fleckenstein do more of my thinking for me.

Allendale, MI

Works Cited

Berthoff, Ann E. *The Mysterious Barricades: Language and Its Limits*. Toronto: U of Toronto P, 1999. Print. Toronto Studies in Semiotics and Communication.
Langer, Susanne K. *Philosophy in a New Key: A Study in the Symbolism of Reason, Rite, and Art*. 3rd ed. Cambridge: Harvard UP, 1957. Print.

Facing the Center: Toward an Identity Politics of One-to-One Mentoring, by Harry C. Denny. Logan: Utah State UP, 2010. 176 pp.

Reviewed by Beth Godbee, University of Wisconsin-Madison

A central contribution of Harry C. Denny's *Facing the Center: Toward an Identity Politics of One-to-One Mentoring* is the attention drawn toward the people involved and the identities they bring to writing conferencing. Writing center researchers have long been interested in and committed to working with people, as articulated in Stephen North's often-cited mission statement: "We are here to talk to writers" (440). Too rarely, however, have we given concerted attention to the identities that writers and writing center staff bring to this talk. As Denny argues, the importance of identity politics for composition teaching cannot be underestimated, as identities impact "the tangible effects of political, economic, social, and cultural forces at play in and often confounding education wherever it's practiced" (7).

Facing the Center succeeds in its aim of bringing research on identity to writing centers. The book offers no easy answers, but instead invites readers to question how our own identity politics influence how we teach writing, understand language, interact with others, and promote success in higher education. To engage in this exploration, Denny uses "face" as an organizing concept, uncovering assumptions of who "we" in writing centers are and how answers to this question shape our pedagogy. Drawing on a number of theorists (e.g., Kenji Yoshino, Cal Logue, and Stuart Hall) and situating identities within broader historical contexts and social movements in the United States, Denny argues that identities are ever-present, yet operate and are read differently depending on context.

One core argument concerns long-standing debates over how to teach writing in socially just ways, specifically whether to encourage assimilation or opposition to mainstream values and rhetorical expectations. Denny maintains assimilation and opposition are false choices that instead reflect "assumptions about power, historical context, and rhetorical need" (112). He proposes a spectrum of options and third possibilities, such as "subversion," or the opportunity for tutors and writers to work together toward rhetorical manipulation of what's expected of them—for example, reimagining assignments or leveraging personal experience where it's not readily allowed. He similarly advocates queer theory as an interpretive method that provides fluidity, hybridity, and liminality in understanding how identity can both oppose and bring into light dominant norms.

Facing the Center is divided into six chapters with five interchapters that put Denny in dialogue with writing consultants from the centers he has directed. The first chapter serves as an introduction to the central concepts of identity politics, face, and one-to-one mentoring. Here Denny shares his own history of civil rights activism in Colorado and HIV/AIDS activism in Philadelphia and tells the story of how he came to see oppression alongside rich possibilities for social change in writing centers. These changes he equates to "micro-shifts" such as those "slippages of tectonic plates" that occur in a slow process of building pressure over time (26). While social change may not be monumental or immediate, it can come about through "micro-successes," culminating in a "tipping point" (8), which an understanding of identity politics helps us work toward.

The middle four chapters address four of the identities, or "faces," writers, consultants, and administrators bring to writing centers. Each provides a theoretical lens for understanding politics associated with that identity: namely, performance for race and ethnicity (chapter 2), capital for class (chapter 3), normalization for sex and gender (chapter 4), and citizenship for nationality (chapter 5). These chapters follow essentially the same order: opening with scenarios and Denny's personal experience and then defining and theorizing the chapter's identity through historical context in the United States. From there, Denny considers what has been expected of marginalized writers who are asked to erase, mute, or cover their identities, and he foregrounds the politics of each chapter's identity in writing centers before closing with parting thoughts.

Many central arguments of the book are initially presented in chapter 2, in which Denny offers his first reading of how identities have been normalized and stigmatized in the United States so that identities are made invisible to those in dominant, majority, or naturalized positions (e.g., white people not seeing race). He critiques the pedagogical expectation that students of color will (want to) "cover," or adopt the rhetorical, linguistic, and behavioral rules of conduct expected by the majority. In doing so, Denny argues that students of color are too-often wedged between assimilation or opposition, a no-win situation that can be countered with subversion.

Next, chapter 3 looks at social class and provides theoretical grounding rooted in cultural studies, drawing particularly from Bourdieu and Foucault. As in chapter 2, Denny describes how middle-class values have been normalized so that working-class students are marked as outsiders. Again, and throughout these four body chapters, Denny critiques a deficit model of education (e.g., efforts to "clean up" drafts and "potty train" novice writers [72]). In contrast to the politics of race, in which legible faces mark students of color as Other, working-class people and sexual minorities are expected (and believed able) to pursue movement from the margin to center, yet with similar costs and loss attached.

Chapter 4 addresses another impasse—this one regarding sex and gender—in which women and sexual minorities walk a line between, on the one hand, being feminized and not taken seriously, and, on the other, being perceived as too tough, outspoken, and therefore, threatening. Denny says that of many "faces," he is made aware daily of this one, as his sexual identity as a gay man challenges dominant codes. Here Denny proposes queering identity politics as a strategy for disrupting and demystifying expectations that are naturalized and for forcing the margin and center to "bleed into the other" (110).

Chapter 5 turns to multilingual writers, both international students and permanent-resident/immigrants, who face overt bias toward language, which reflects broader concepts of citizenship in the United States, specifically ideas of "who we're *not*" and "who we'll *allow*" (123). Putting research on citizenship and second language acquisition into conversation, Denny teases out how the myths of national identity and language together exert pressure for multilingual writers to attempt to pass or cover, pressures that feed into narratives of "fixing" L2 writers' texts and parallel similar pressures facing students of color, working-class students, women, and sexual minorities. In contrast to "fixing," Denny suggests teaching writing through a strategic stance that again gives writers the agency to choose subversion, while also educating faculty about Global English.

As the conclusion, chapter 6 uses the understandings of identity developed in chapters 2-5 to raise proactive questions about the "face" of writing centers, both as a professional identity and as a unit or site on campus. Chapter 6 concludes by unpacking the relationship of individual and institutional identity, highlighting the position of writing centers as marginal or central to their institutions, and questioning what subversion could offer writing center professionals.

To be honest, I came to the book a bit skeptical about this chapter organization. How could Denny pull apart the intersections of identities and the logic of oppression into discreet chapters? By the end of chapter 3, however, Denny had convinced me, a skeptical reader, of the importance of this organization—both its predictability and its repetition of core concepts, including the push-pull of assimilation and opposition and the choices and demands of covering and subverting. This repetition of key themes helps to reiterate issues of power and privilege across identities and to show how individual identities are part of larger institutional inequities. Further, the reiteration demonstrates the consistency in identity politics and helps us understand how some identities are consistently privileged, while others are excluded and Othered. The organization additionally allows Denny to position himself within each identity, which models for readers the reflective personal inquiry he advocates and strengthens the theory he builds through narrative authoethnography.

In total, *Facing the Center* reminds readers that issues of power and privilege, the center and margin, assimilation and opposition are central to the mission of writing centers and composition teaching, as they are central to higher education. I can certainly see adopting *Facing the Center* in courses on composition pedagogy, writing center studies, and peer tutoring practice. Because Denny introduces readers to identity politics and how they are so intricate within institutions, he also makes an important call for educators to consider deeply our own identities and those of writers. In doing so, he draws attention to writing centers as "sites *par excellance*" for making "local, material and individual all the larger forces at play that confound, impede, and make possible education in institutions" (6). For the broader field of Composition and Rhetoric, this book highlights the social change possibilities in writing centers, important sites in which identity politics are enacted, contested, and subverted on an everyday basis. For writing center practitioners, the book is a call to action, a call I hope more and more writing centers take up in their missions.

Madison, WI

Works Cited

North, Stephen. "The Idea of the Writing Center." *College English* 46.5 (Sept. 1984): 433-446. Print.

Working in the Archives: Practical Research Methods for Rhetoric and Composition, edited by Alexis E. Ramsey, Wendy B. Sharer, Barbara L'Eplattenier, and Lisa S. Mastrangelo. Carbondale: Southern Illinois UP, 2010. 317 pp.

Reviewed by Marta Hess, Georgia State University

Working in the Archives offers a valuable assessment of and guide to the increasingly complex endeavors of archival research. The editors state that this collection, which includes eighteen full-length essays, seven interviews, a general introduction, and an introduction to the interviews, "will help scholars find, access, analyze, and compile the archival materials upon which diverse histories of rhetoric and composition might continue to be built" (4). Indeed, while the book accomplishes all of its intended goals, it also provides the reader a welcoming community of scholars from which to learn and feel part of, asking questions that allow us to think about our work in different ways. Notably, the short interviews/essays interspersed with the longer, more academically traditional selections include both novice and experienced researchers into a group whose enthusiasm for and dedication to their subjects are obvious. The contributors to *Working in the Archives* invite both beginners and expert researchers into their worlds. The collection informs and delights on several levels.

Although the editors state that they have written this book "for the scholar new to the archive in the hope of helping prevent archive fever [a term they attribute to Carolyn Steedman] while at the same time enabling them to more systematically 'play' in the archives" (3), the essays included will be as valuable to more experienced researchers as well and to scholars in all disciplines. Not only those in Rhetoric and Composition, but those working on projects in other areas of the humanities and social sciences will find advice, encouragement, and new ways to think about archival research in this collection.

The book is divided into four parts: "General Information for Using Archives," "Accessing the Archives," "Working with/through Archival Material," and "Creating the Archive as Research Process." In the longer essays, authors explore current issues in archival research as well as recount their own stories of their experiences in the archives. The shorter interviews/ personal essays interspersed throughout the text present the reader with the sometimes intangible aspects of archival research, and several of them, such as Peter Mortensen's "'I Had a Hunch'" and Kathryn Fitzgerald's "'I'm Open to Whatever I Discover,'" point to the serendipitous nature of the work we do as researchers.

Cheryl Glenn and Jessica Enoch's essay "Invigorating Historiographic Practices in Rhetoric and Composition Studies," appears first in the book and indeed, the word "invigorating" appropriately describes the entire collection. Glenn and Enoch acknowledge the challenges and opportunities for work in the archives and the need to reconsider the ways that we conduct research. They encourage readers to "broaden the scope of historiographic methods" (12), using examples of Glenn's work on classical women and Enoch's on female teachers and their African American, Native American, and Chicano/a students. The lack of available information they encountered forced each of them to consider different ways to obtain the information they needed. Lynée Lewis Gaillet's essay, "Archival Survival: Navigating Historical Research," compares the work of the researcher to that of girl detective Nancy Drew – an analogy Gaillet develops as she sets out a practical guide for those conducting archival research, navigating through what can be a mysterious quest for information. She suggests, for example, that researchers visit local collections in order to become familiar with the process, and she offers advice on applying for grants, and shares ways to navigate through the archival maze. At the same time she raises provocative questions about the researcher's construction of her or his ethos. Additionally, Gaillet offers advice about how to evaluate findings in order for researchers to be "effective, scholarly storytellers" (29).

In part 2, "Accessing the Archives," Sammie L. Morris and Shirley K. Rose's "Invisible Hands: Recognizing Archivists' Work to Make Records Accessible" grants the reader an entrée into the work that archivists carry out before we as researchers even see the documents in a collection. Under Morris's guidance, Rose processed the academic papers of James Berlin, documents ranging from 1978 to 1994. The authors reveal issues that we as researchers may have given little consideration such as the collection's provenance and its original order. They also raise issues about the hand of the archivist in altering original materials. For example, Rose (after consulting with Morris) removed the rusting spiral from one of Berlin's notebooks and the cardboard backings from notepads in order to preserve the pages. In "Viewing the Archives: The Hidden and the Digital," Alexis E. Ramsey raises timely questions concerning the allocation of limited funds, how those funds are spent, and the ways in which those financial decisions impact scholars, noting especially the problem for researchers who cannot access collections that are hidden or underprocessed due to lack of funding. Moreover, and especially important in our digitalized culture, Ramsey considers the benefits and drawbacks of technology and archival research, and raises fascinating questions about what we lose by using only digitized documents and images. Although a dress might look beautiful on screen, for example, if we cannot "hear how the fabric sounds as it moves, or smell the fabric, or cannot observe the rips, stains, or stitching up close" it loses its "uniqueness" (85).

In part 3, several of the essays raise questions of ethics and the objectivity/subjectivity we must account for in our work. Katherine E. Tirabassi begins her essay "Journeying into the Archives: Exploring the Pragmatics of Archival Research" by describing a typical day of her dissertation research, noting both the random and organic natures of the process. By recording her observations of the process itself, Tirabassi determined four research principles: selectivity, cross-referencing, categorization, and closure, that influenced her "evolving understanding of the archives" (171), and that are valuable for planning and organizing new projects. Liz Rohan, in "The Personal as Method and Place as Archives: A Synthesis," calls to our attention the ethical dilemmas involved in researching and writing about the late nineteenth/early twentieth-century missionary, Janette Miller, whom at times she "neither understood nor respected" (232). With the help of photographs and maps Rohan utilizes the city of Detroit as her archive as she travels its streets searching for and finding the neighborhood where Miller lived.

Part 4, "Creating the Archive as Research Process," contains three essays that explore the relationship between using the archives and creating an archive of one's own. The last essay, "Autobiography of an Archivist" by Nan Johnson, beautifully illustrates the connections between researcher and archivist. Johnson recounts her ongoing experiences searching for, collecting, and organizing material related to rhetoric and gender in nineteenth-century North America as she assembles her own archive. As she looks for the correlation among the various categories of texts she collected, she experiences a revelation when she arranges them into a wheel pattern and realizes that there is no center. We share her excitement as she identifies what that hub should be, and using her "Archival Wheel" sees the collections in her archives "with new eyes" (296).

Working in the Archives would be an excellent text for graduate and undergraduate classes in bibliographic or archival research, providing them with a solid foundation from which to begin their work. Additionally, because it offers new ways to think about theory and process, all scholars who plan to conduct archival research will benefit from the essays in the text.

The editors have selected essays that highlight the sense of community that archivists develop despite the solitary nature of their work, and the book demonstrates the value of collaboration in this area; not only is it edited by four prominent archival scholars, but several of the essays are co-written. Their decision to include personal memoirs creates a sense of familiarity and collegiality as though one were working with a mentor, encouraging those of us who might become overwhelmed with the amount of material available or bemoan the lack of resources relevant to our projects. Starting archival research is akin to beginning a journey for which some of us have a definite destination in mind and others look forward to what they might find along the way. This collection helps guide the researcher through this exciting territory.

Atlanta, GA

Contributors

Hollie Adams received her Masters Degree in English and Creative Writing from the University of Windsor and is currently pursuing her doctorate in English and Creative Writing at the University of Calgary.

Margaret Artman is an associate professor of English and Writing Program Director at Western Oregon University. She teaches composition, news writing, public relations writing, and business and technical writing. In addition to information literacy and course-integrated library instruction, her research interests include writing program administration, teacher training, and assessment.

Jennifer Bay is assistant professor of English at Purdue University where she teaches courses in professional writing, new media, and rhetorical theory. Her work has appeared in journals such as *JAC, College English*, and *Programmatic Perspectives*, as well as in edited collections.

Jessica Enoch is associate professor of English at the University of Pittsburgh. Her research and teaching interests are concerned with rhetorical education, public writing, literacy studies, feminist rhetorical history, and historiography. She published *Refiguring Rhetorical Education: Women Teaching African American, Native American, and Chicano/a Students, 1865-1911* in 2008.

Erica Frisicaro-Pawlowski is an assistant professor of English at Daemen College, where she serves as Writing Coordinator and teaches basic, first-year, and advanced composition. Her research interests center on issues of disciplinary history and professional development in Composition.

Brian Jackson earned a Ph.D. from the University of Arizona in Rhetoric, Composition, and the Teaching of English. He serves as Associate Coordinator of University Writing at Brigham Young University.

Dale Jacobs teaches and directs the Composition program at the University of Windsor. He edited *The Myles Horton Reader* and co-edited (with Laura Micciche) *A Way to Move*. His articles have appeared in such journals as *JAC, College Composition and Communication, English Journal, Biography*, and *Composition Studies*.

Leigh A. Jones is an Assistant Professor of English at Hunter College of the City University of New York. In addition to performance studies and multimodal composing practices in the college writing classroom, her research interests include rhetorics of nationalism and masculinity.

Robert Monge is an assistant professor at Western Oregon University where he is the Instruction and Outreach Librarian. He also teaches a Designing Web-Based Tutorials and a Freshman Year Experience course. His research interests focus on how people learn how to use information in scholarly and professional settings.

Janine Morris recently graduated with her Master's Degree in English Language and Literature from the University of Windsor. She plans to begin pursuing her doctorate in Composition and English Literature in Fall 2011.

M.A. and Ph.D. in Rhetoric and Writing

As a student in rhetoric and writing at UTEP, you'll not only study cross-cultural rhetorics, *you'll live them.*

Our program offers
- A unique location on the U.S.-Mexico border
- Faculty mentors with expertise in global rhetorics, second language writing, digital literacies, and rhetoric and technology
- Community engagement in a multicultural setting
- Experience in areas such as curriculum design and administrative work
- Opportunities for students to explore their own interests through concentration areas
- Graduate assistantships and financial aid

To learn more about our program, faculty, and students please follow the Rhetoric and Writing link at

www.utep.edu/english

The University of Texas at El Paso
500 W. University Ave.
El Paso, TX 79968
915-747-5000

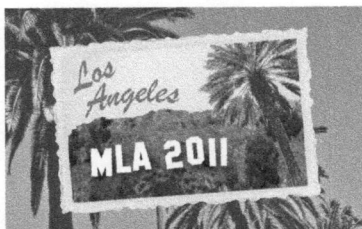

www.ingramcontent.com/pod-product-compliance
Lightning Source LLC
Chambersburg PA
CBHW020614270326
41927CB00005B/337